Simone Sereni

I0408570

Halloween
Skull Party

A Burst of Creativity for Your Halloween

Coloring Book

ISBN: 9798857404560

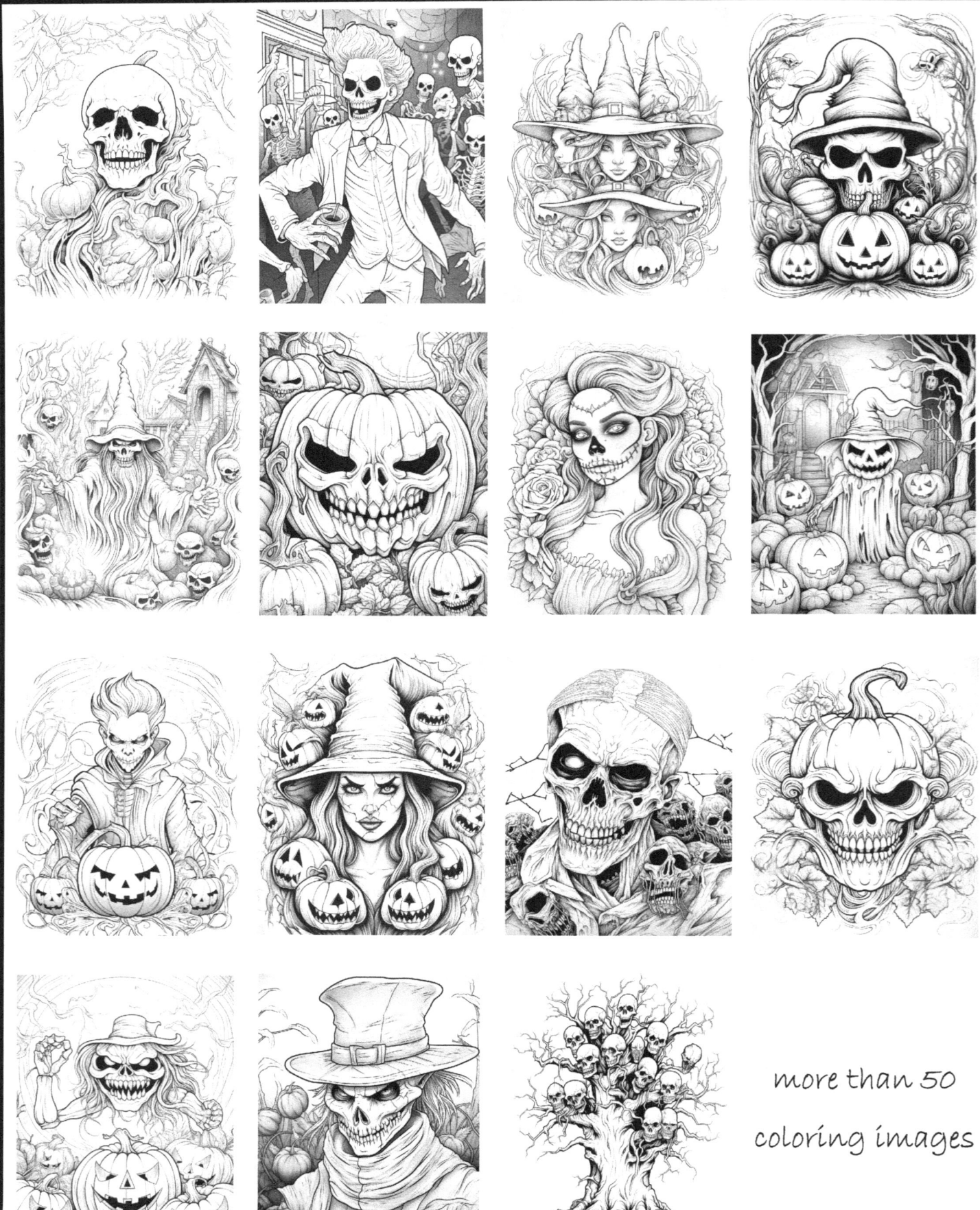

more than 50
coloring images

Color Test Page

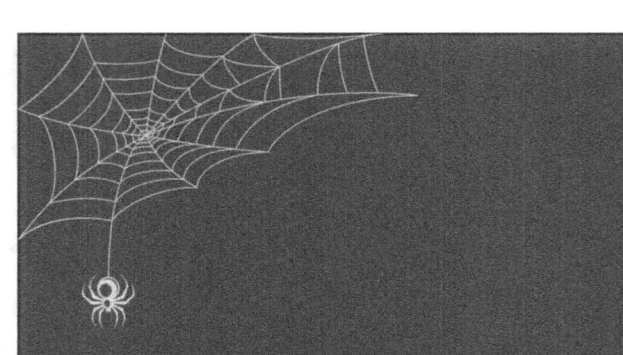

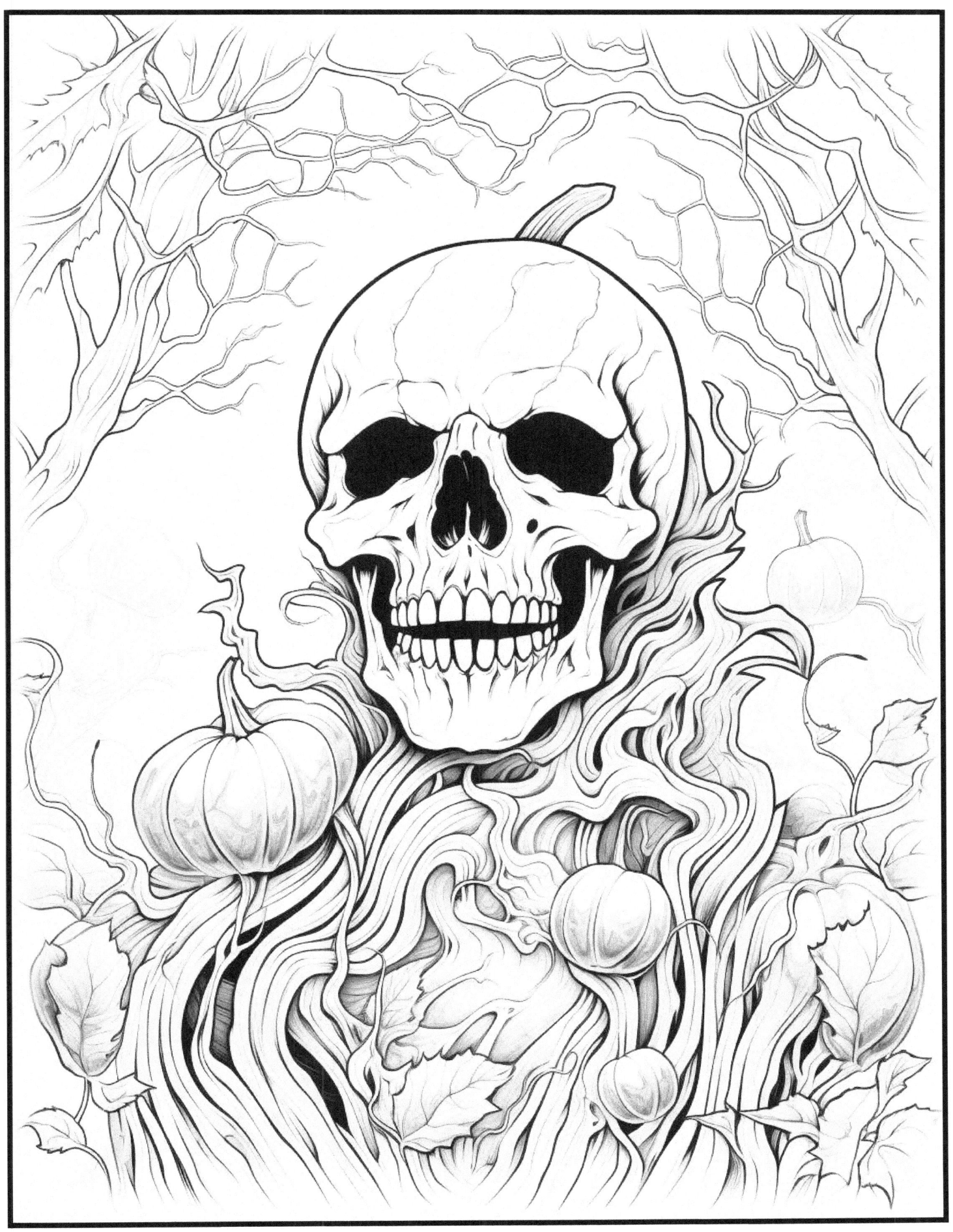

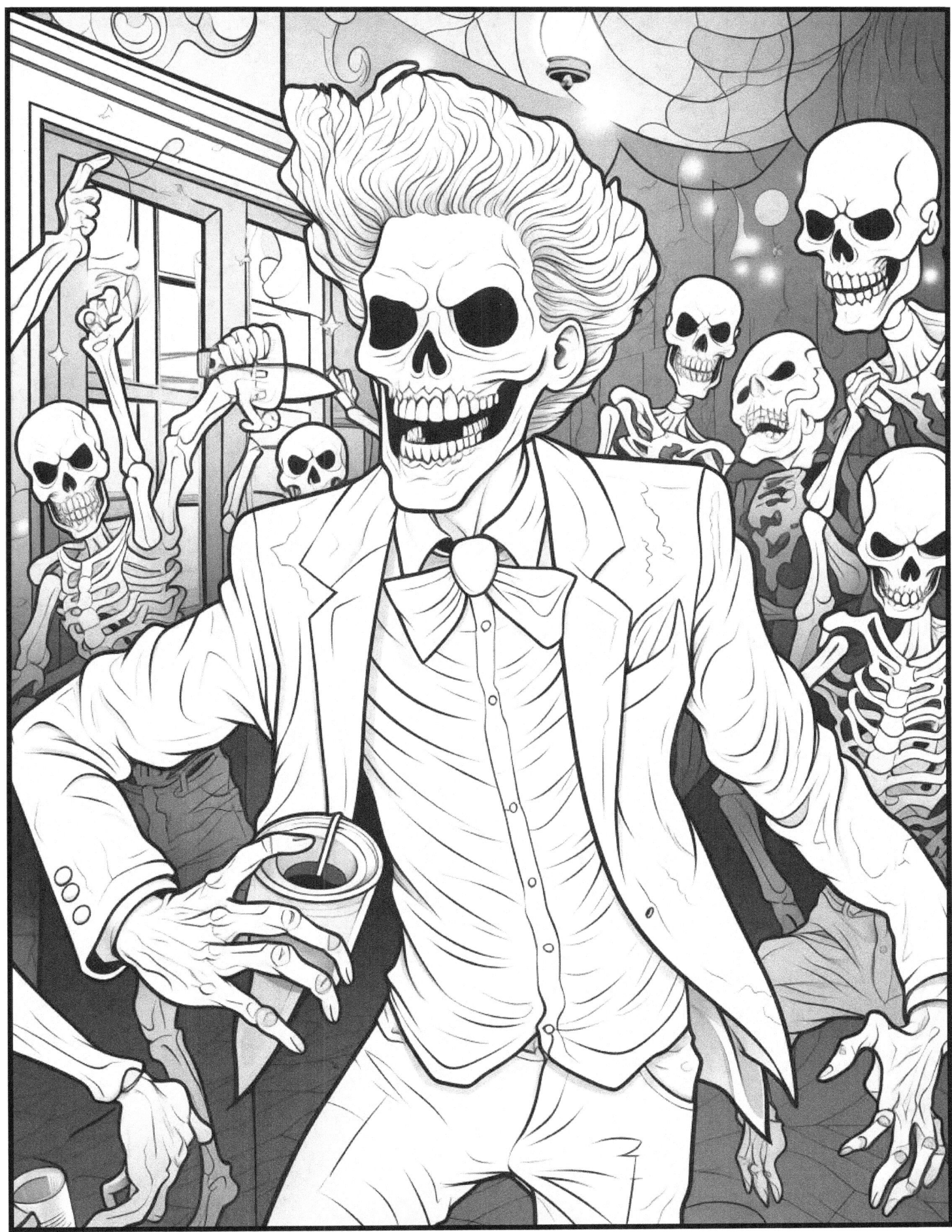

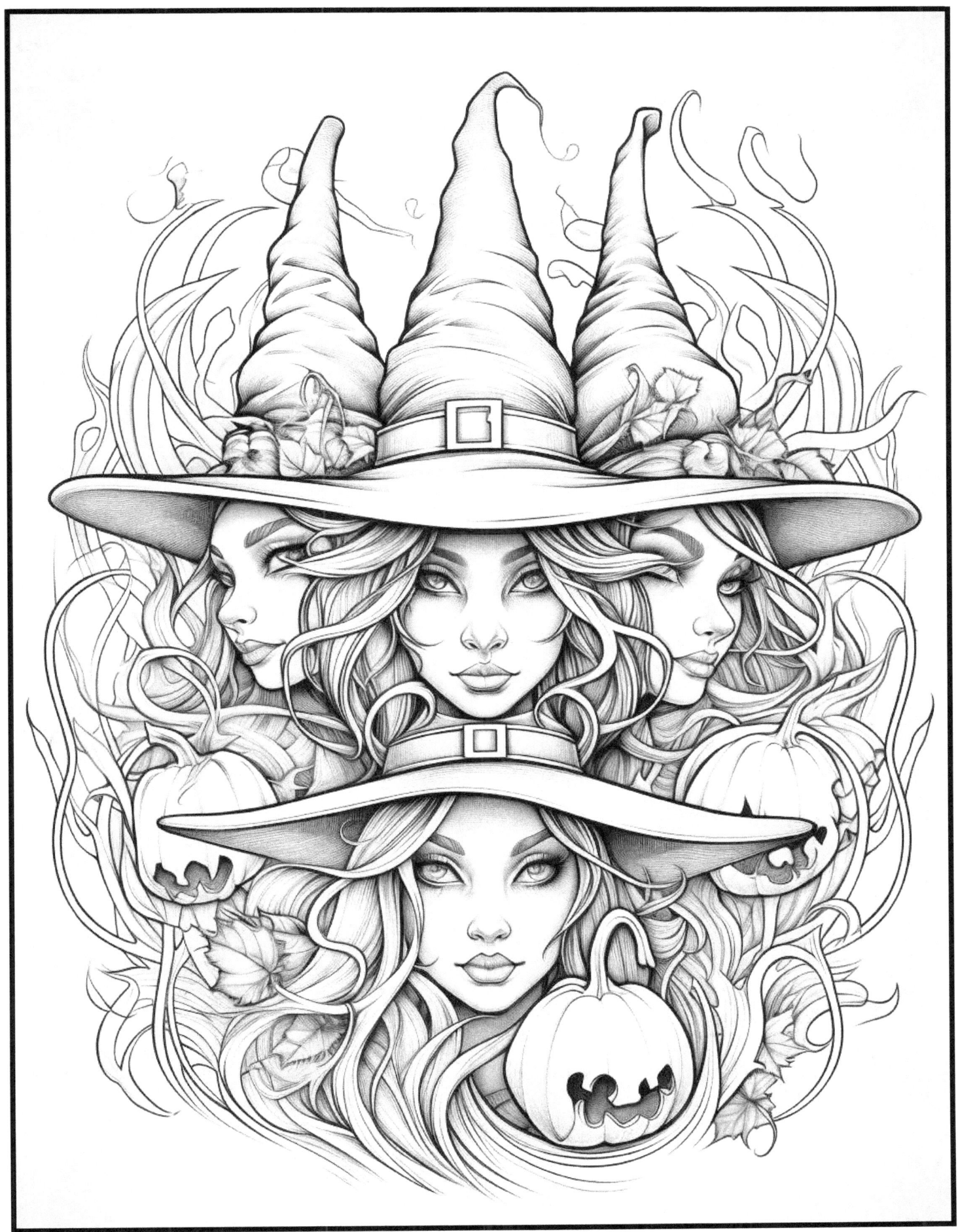

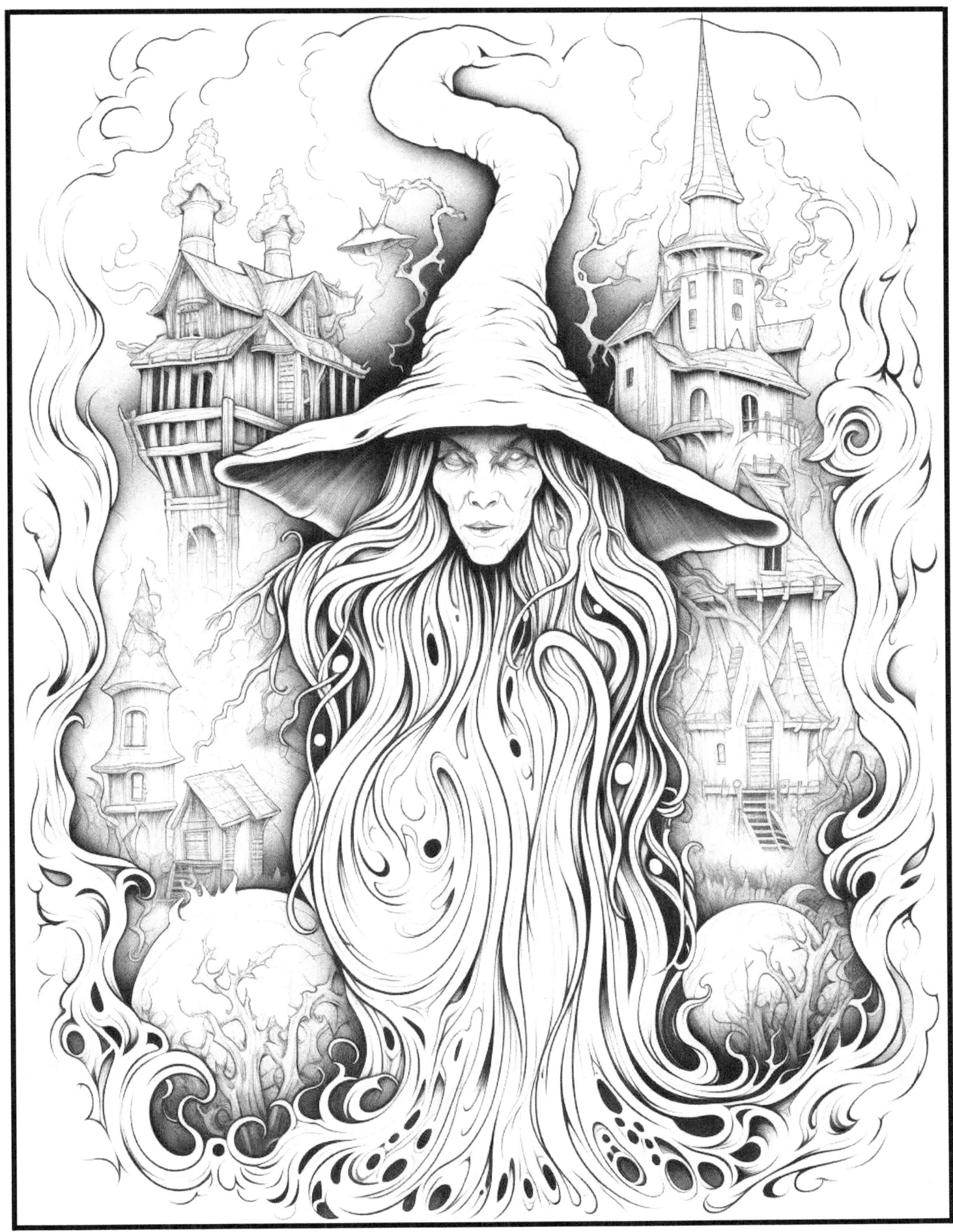

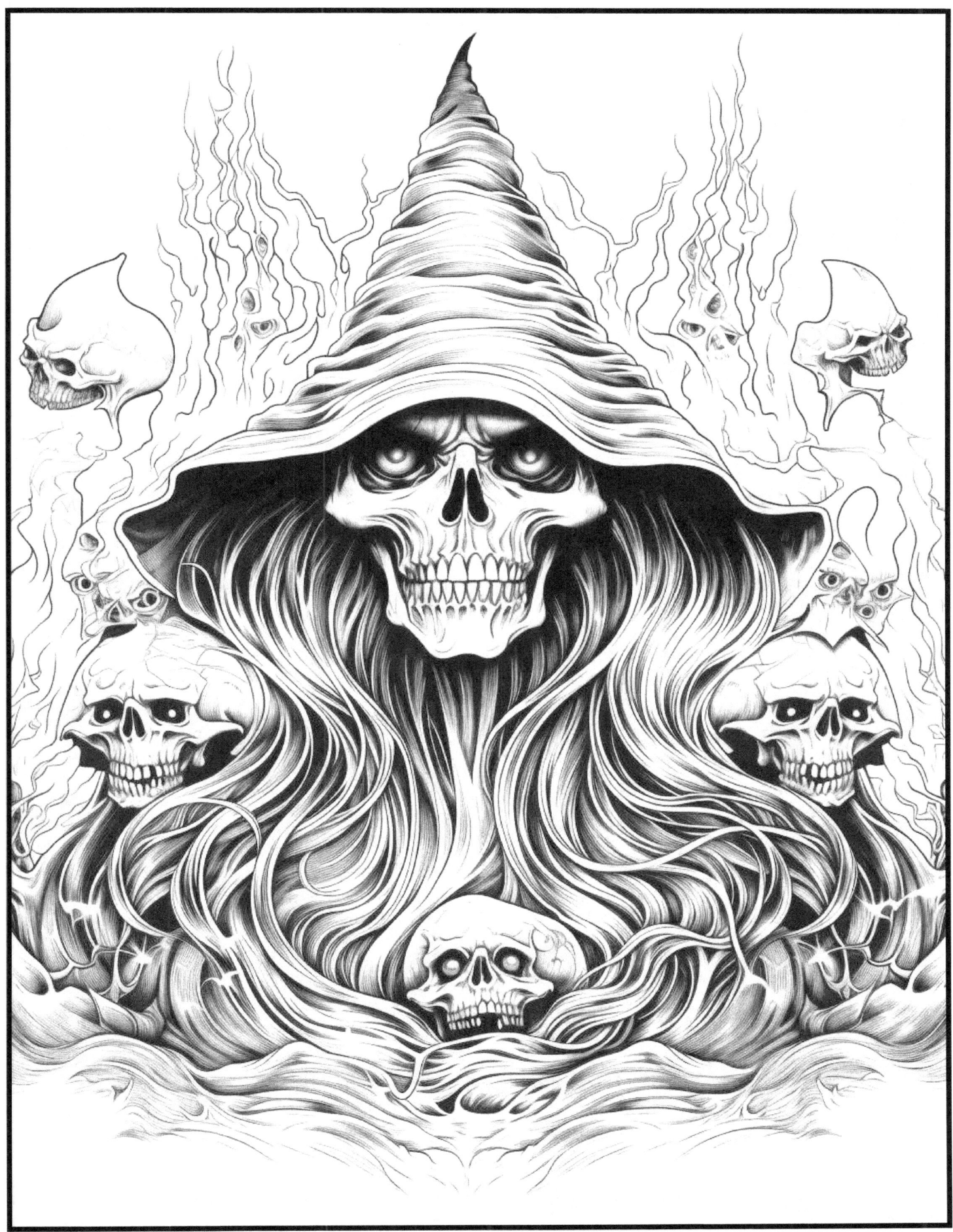

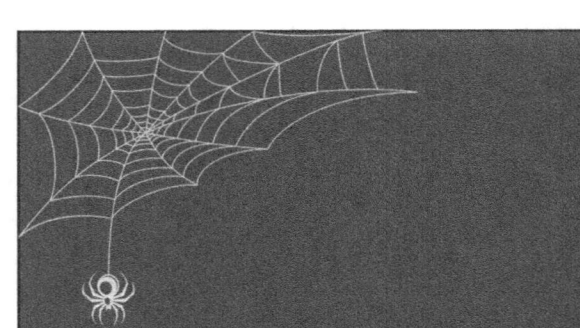

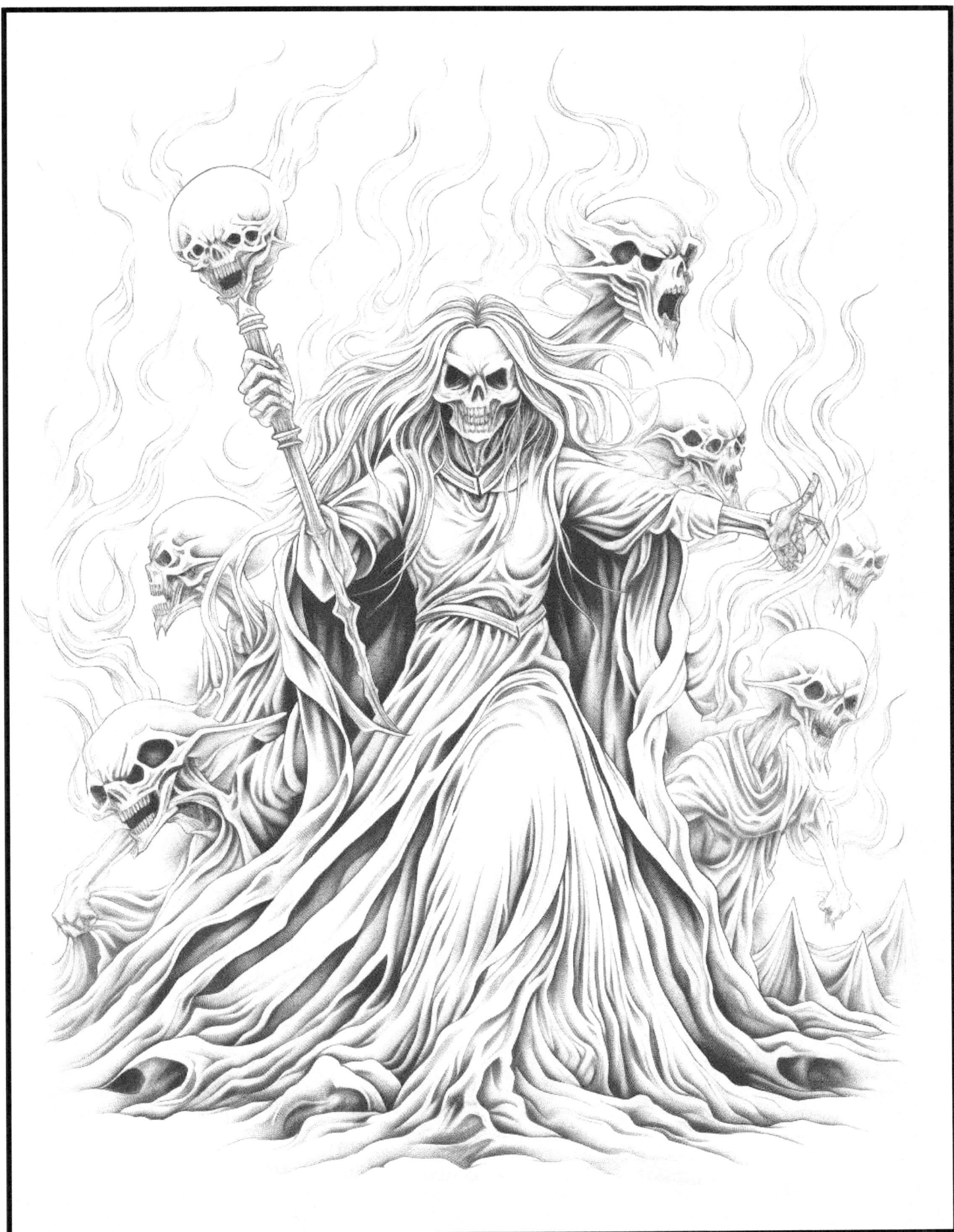

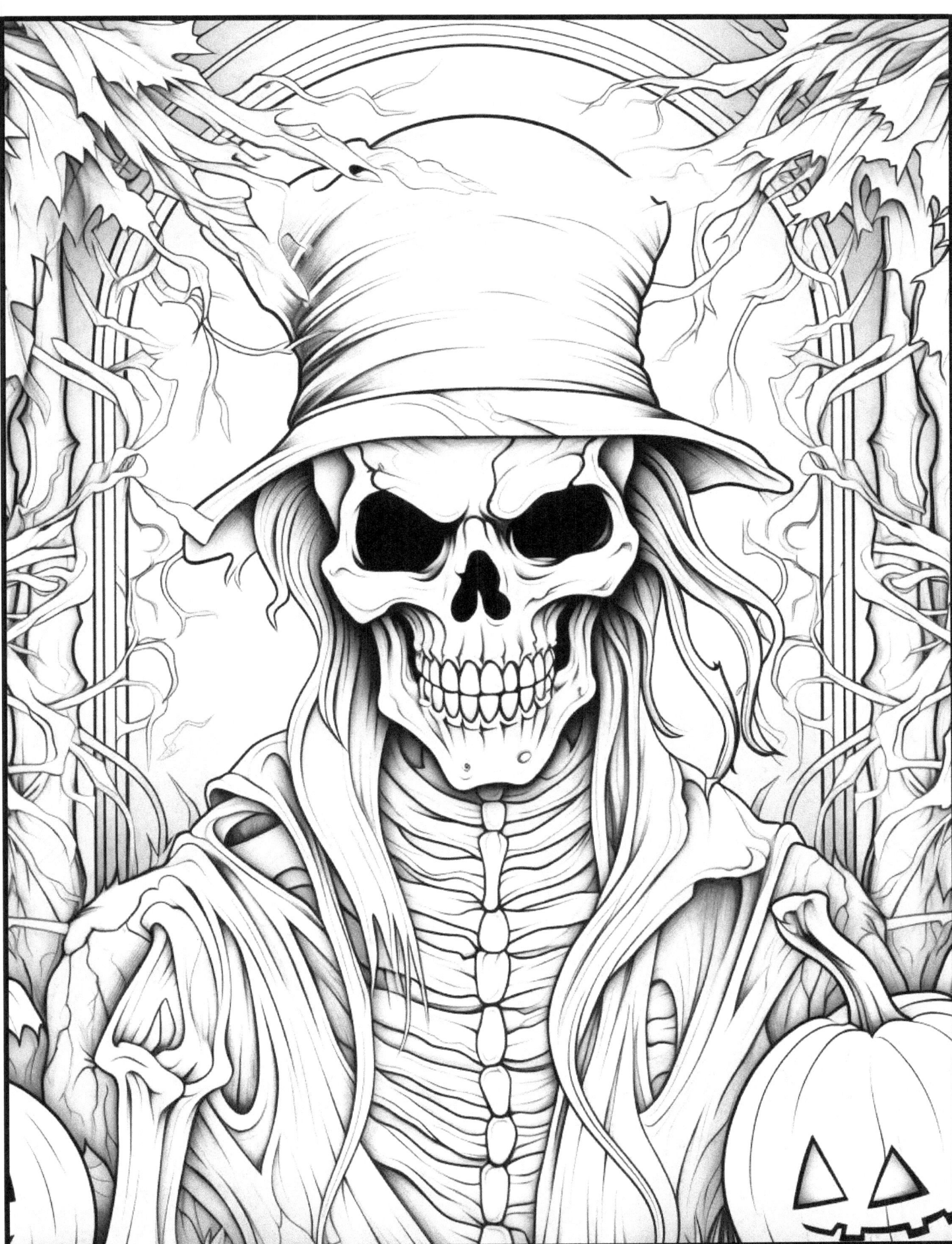

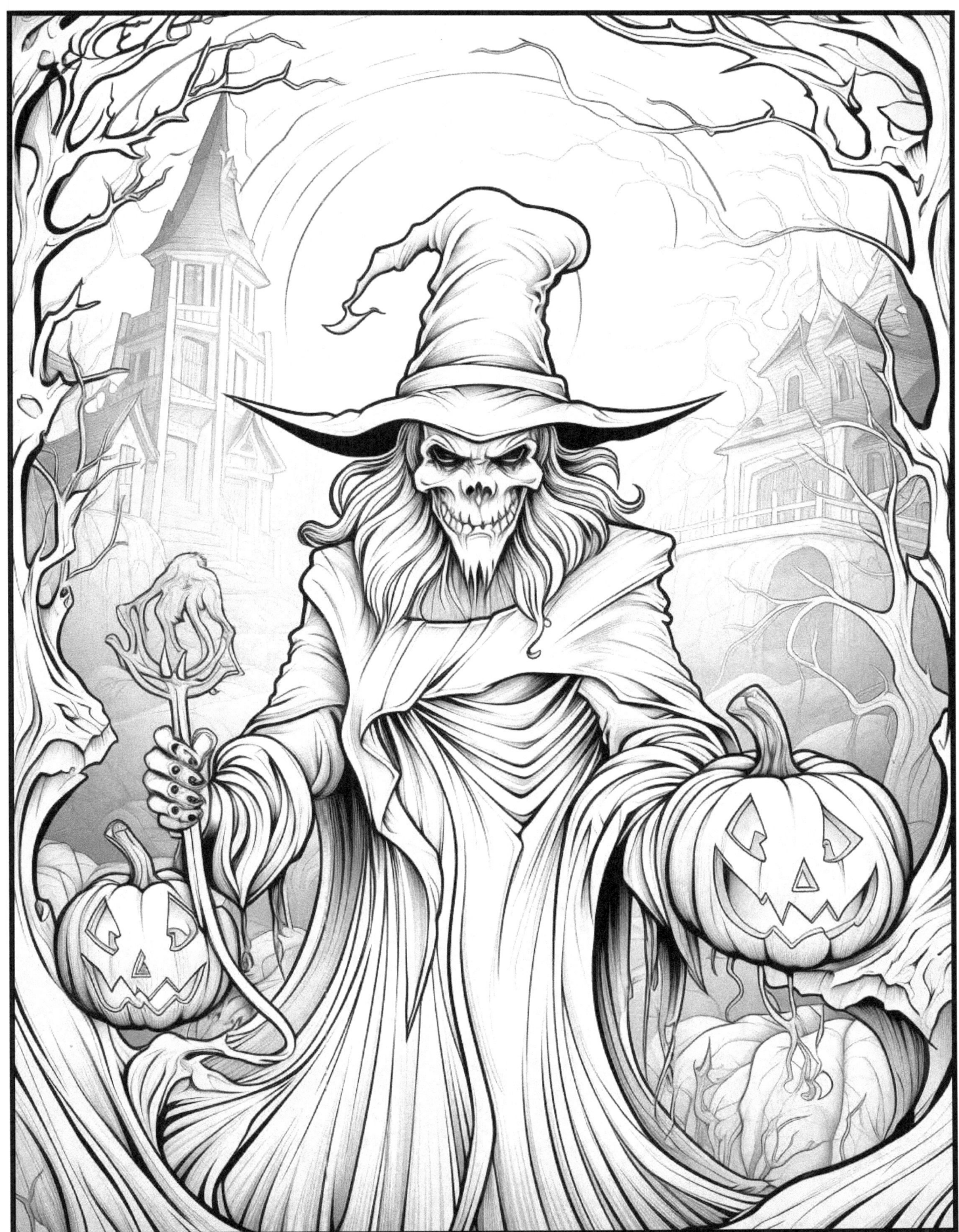

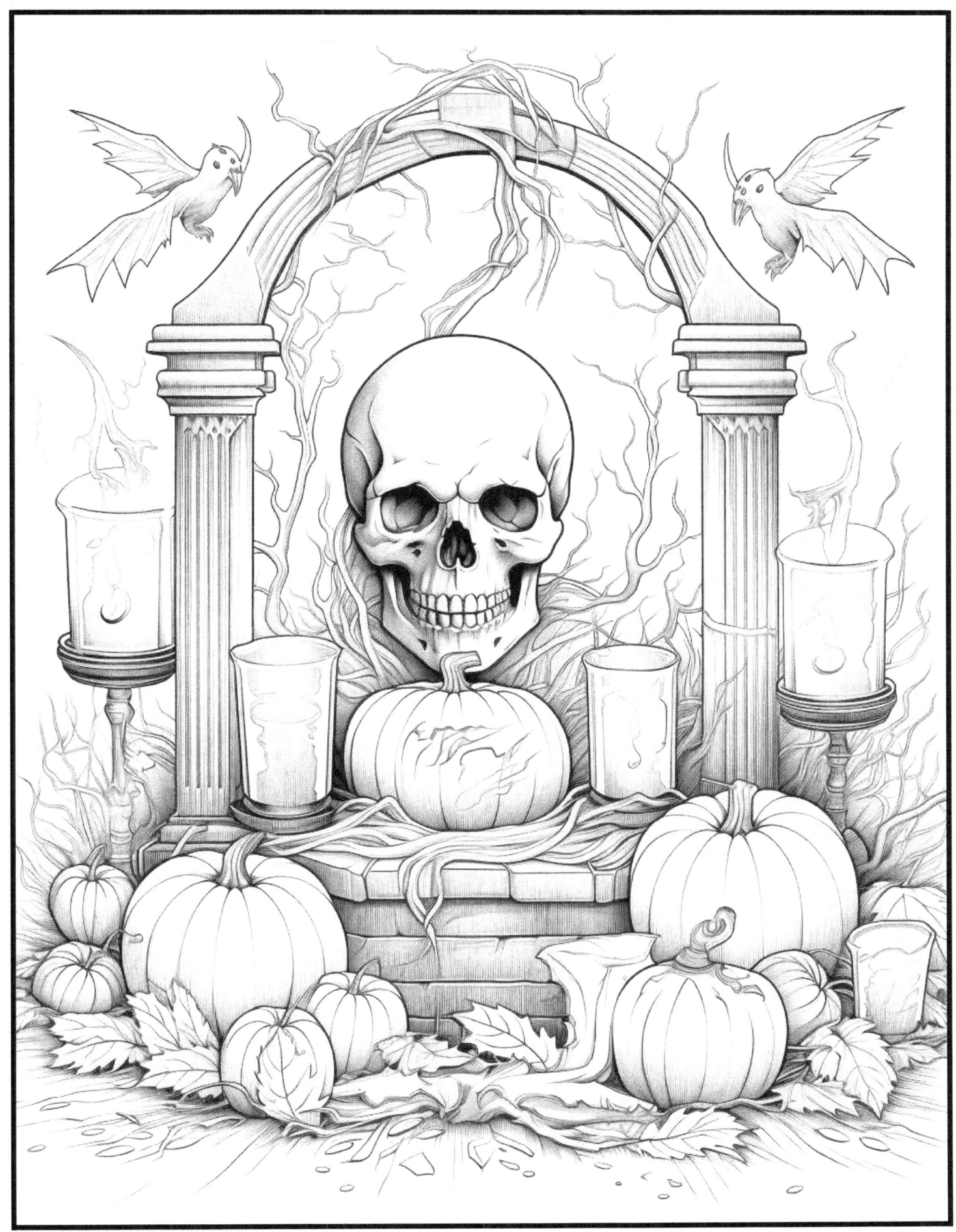

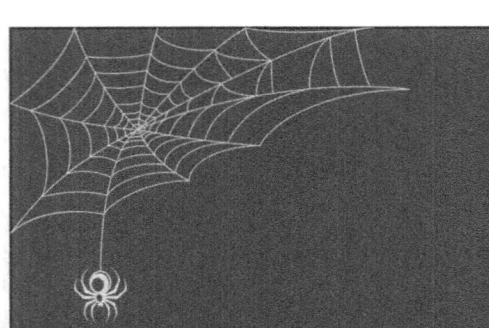

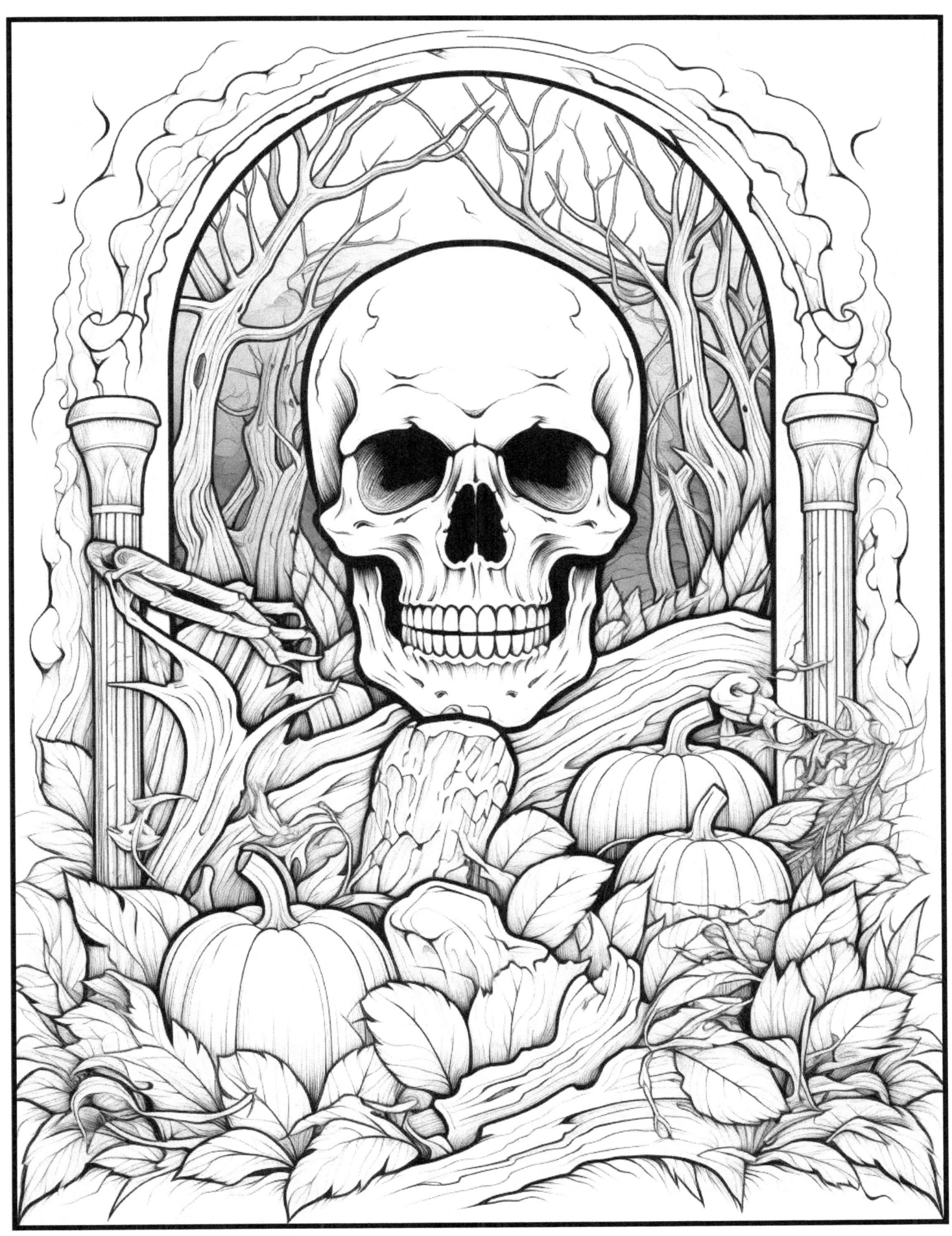

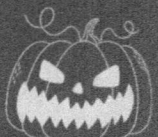

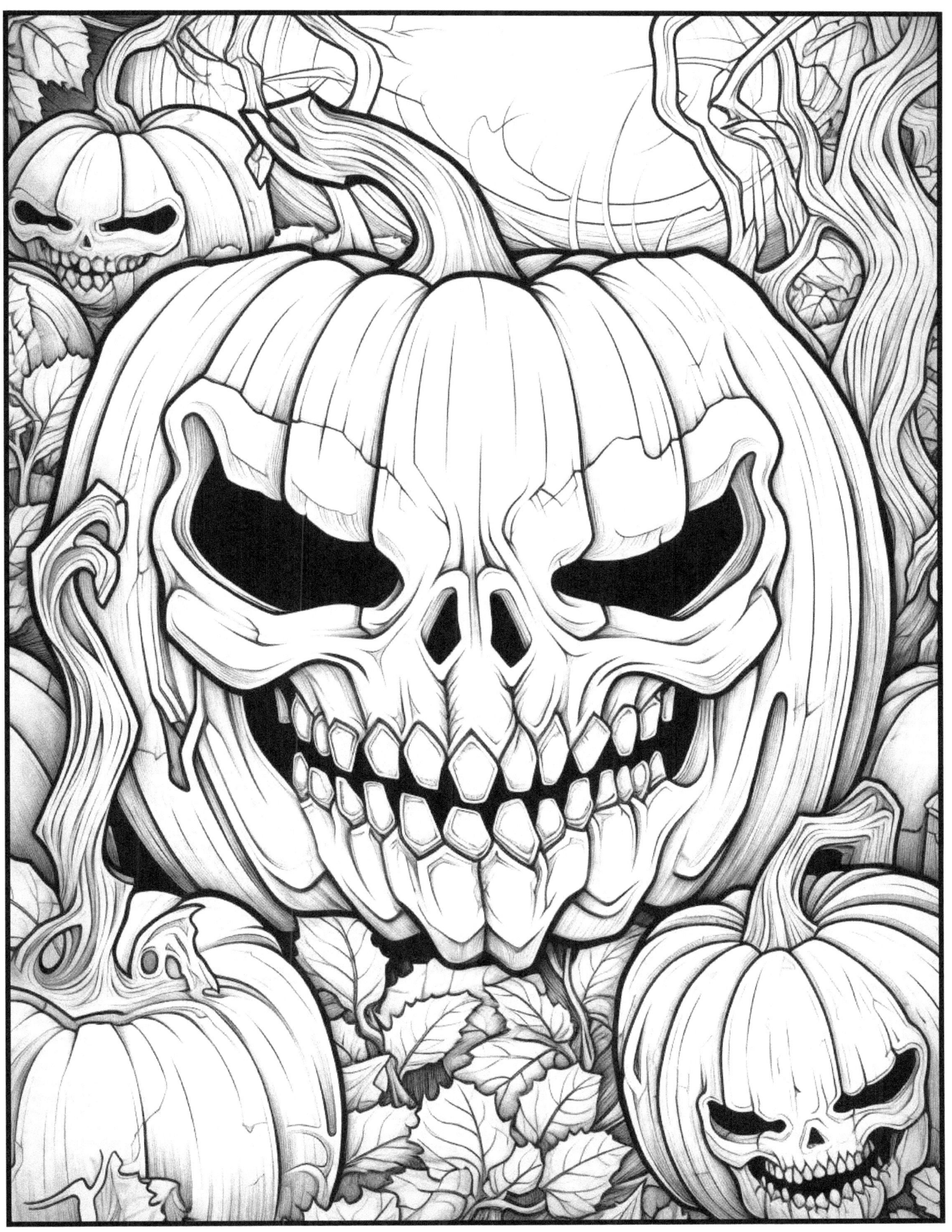

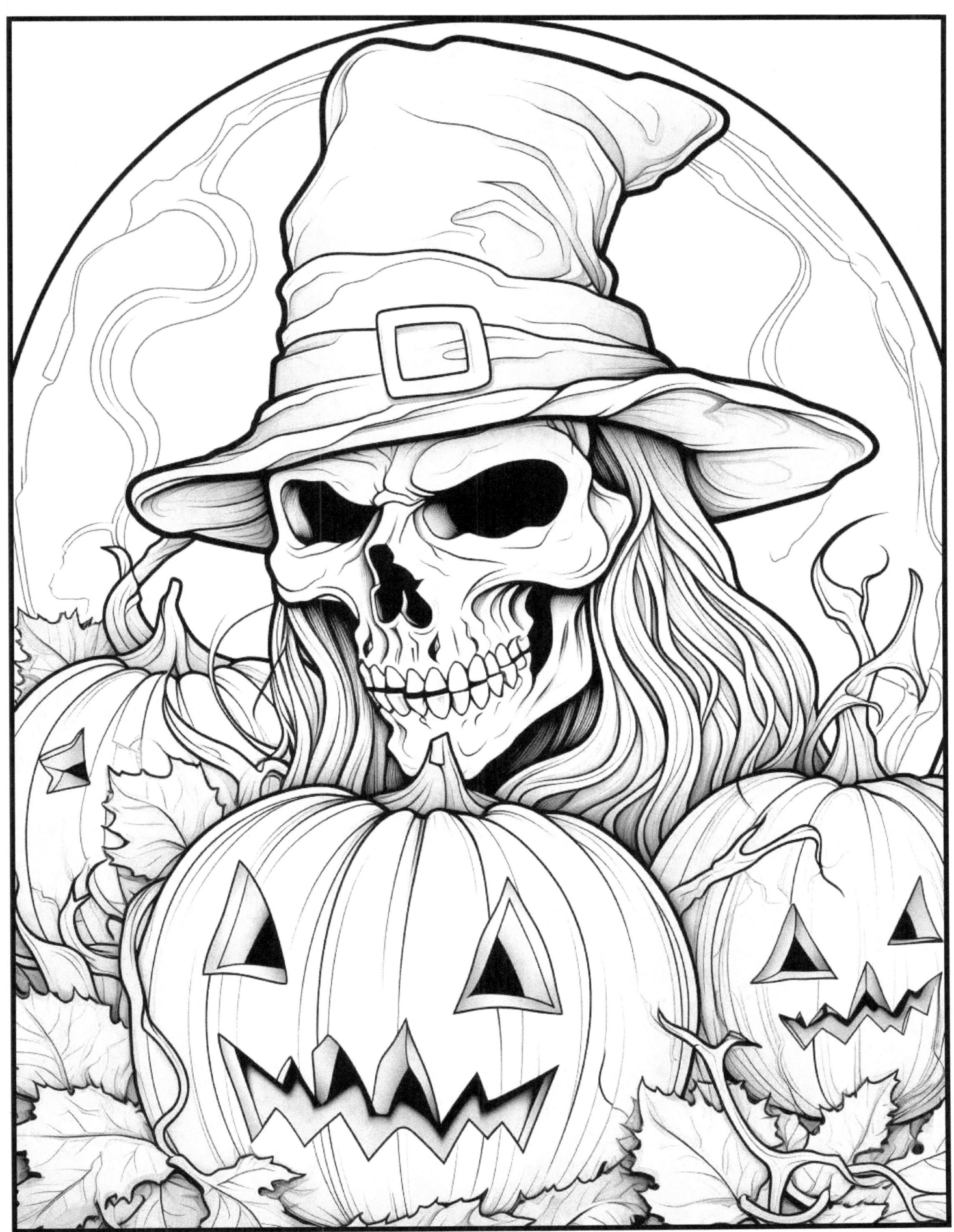

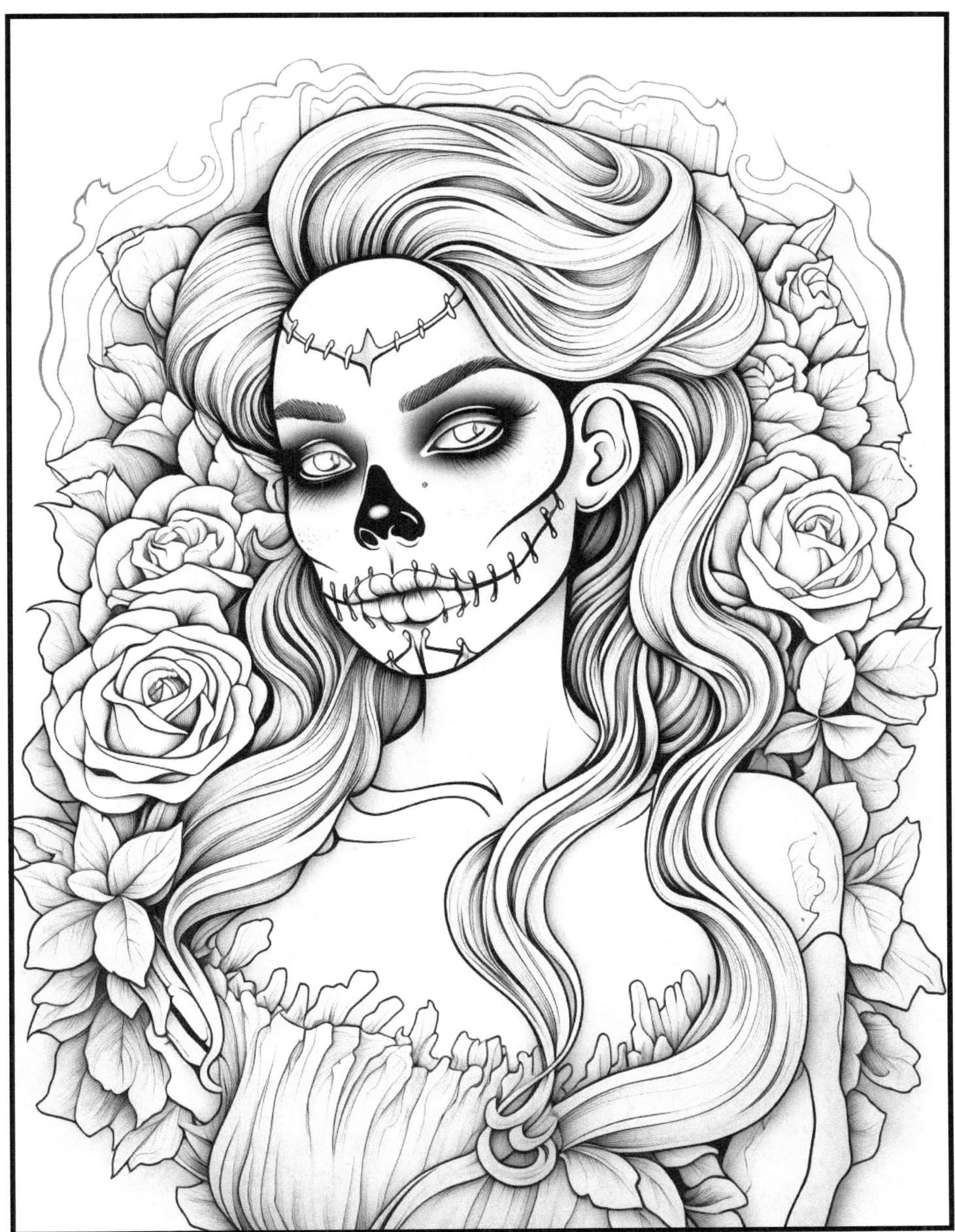

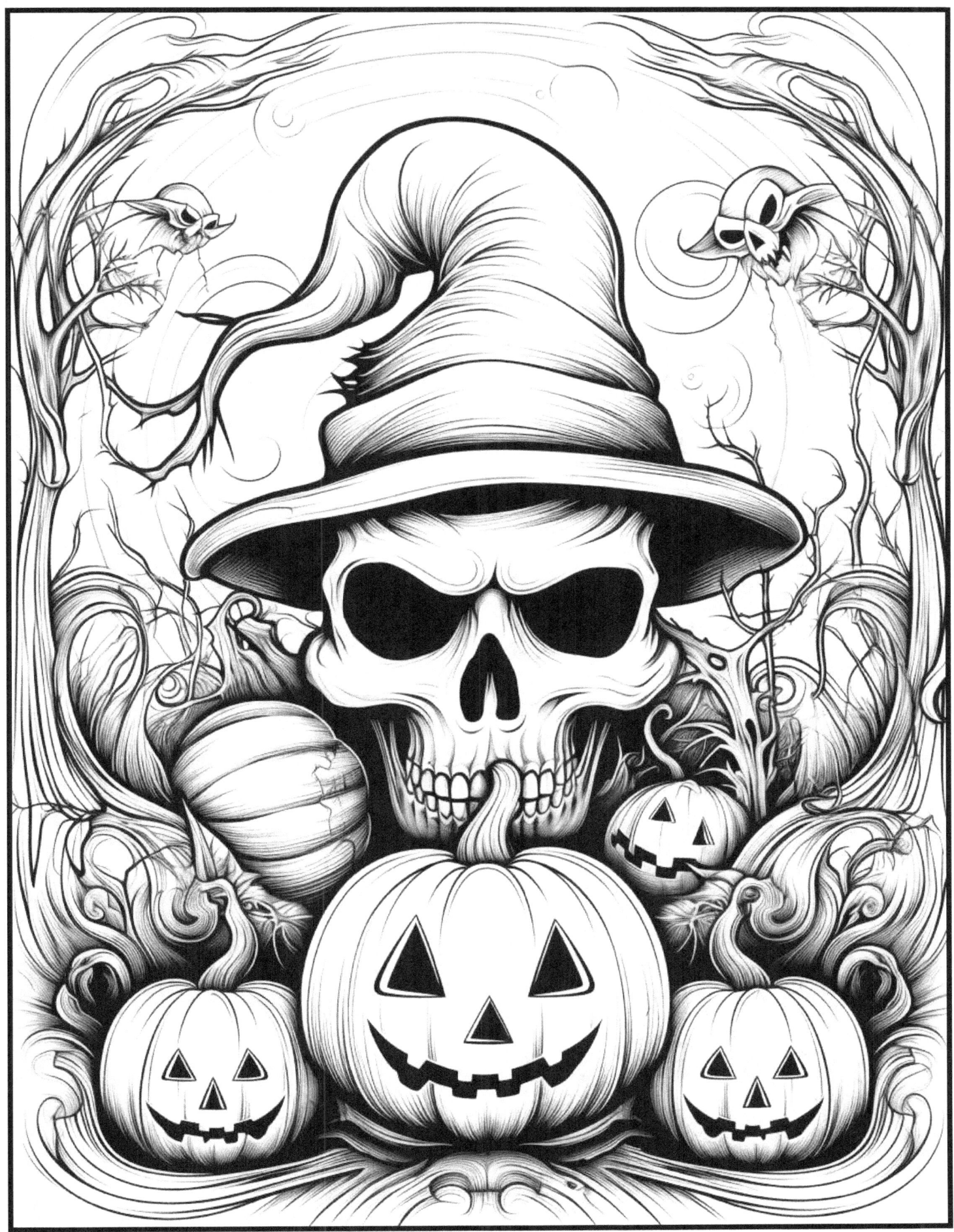

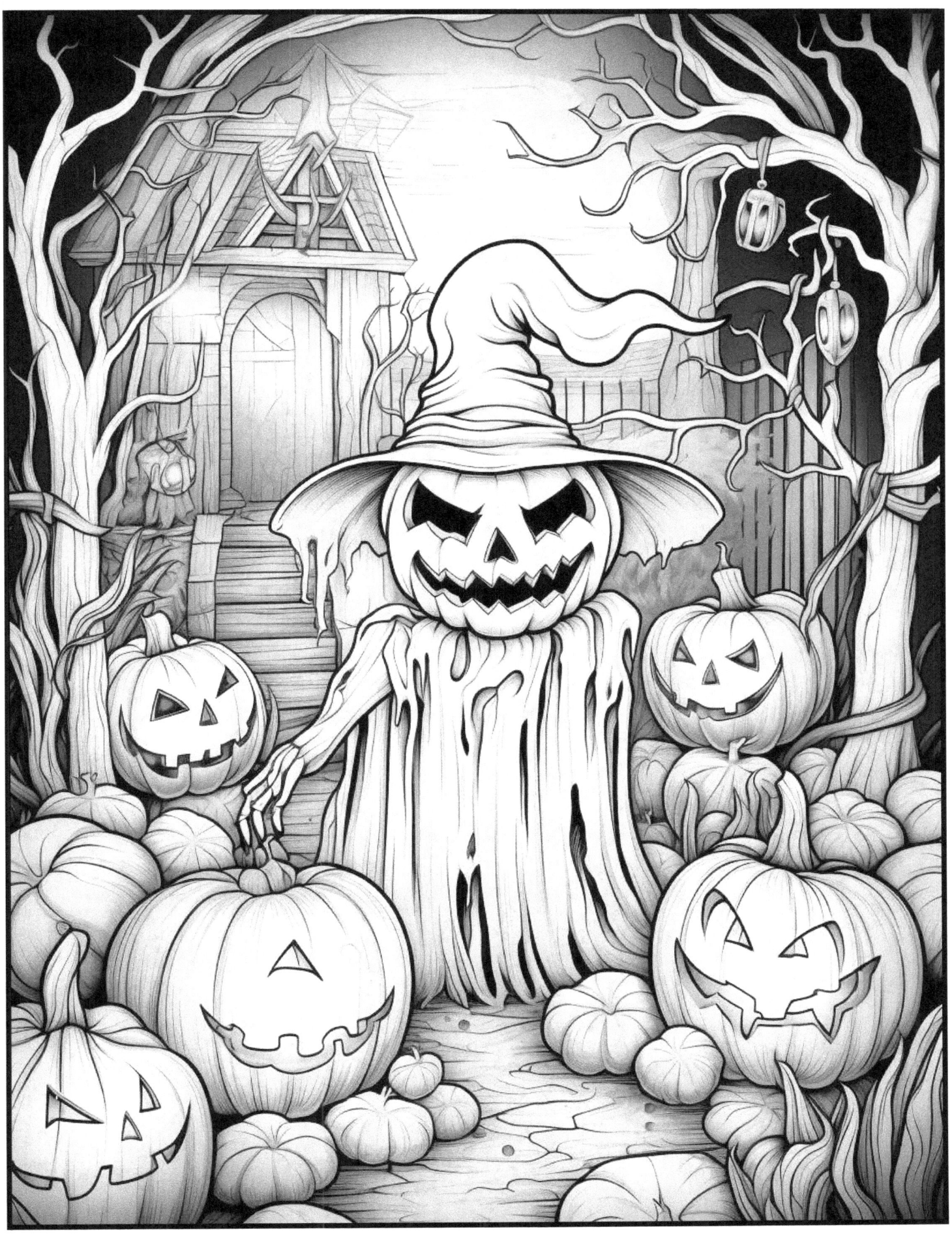

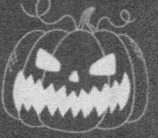

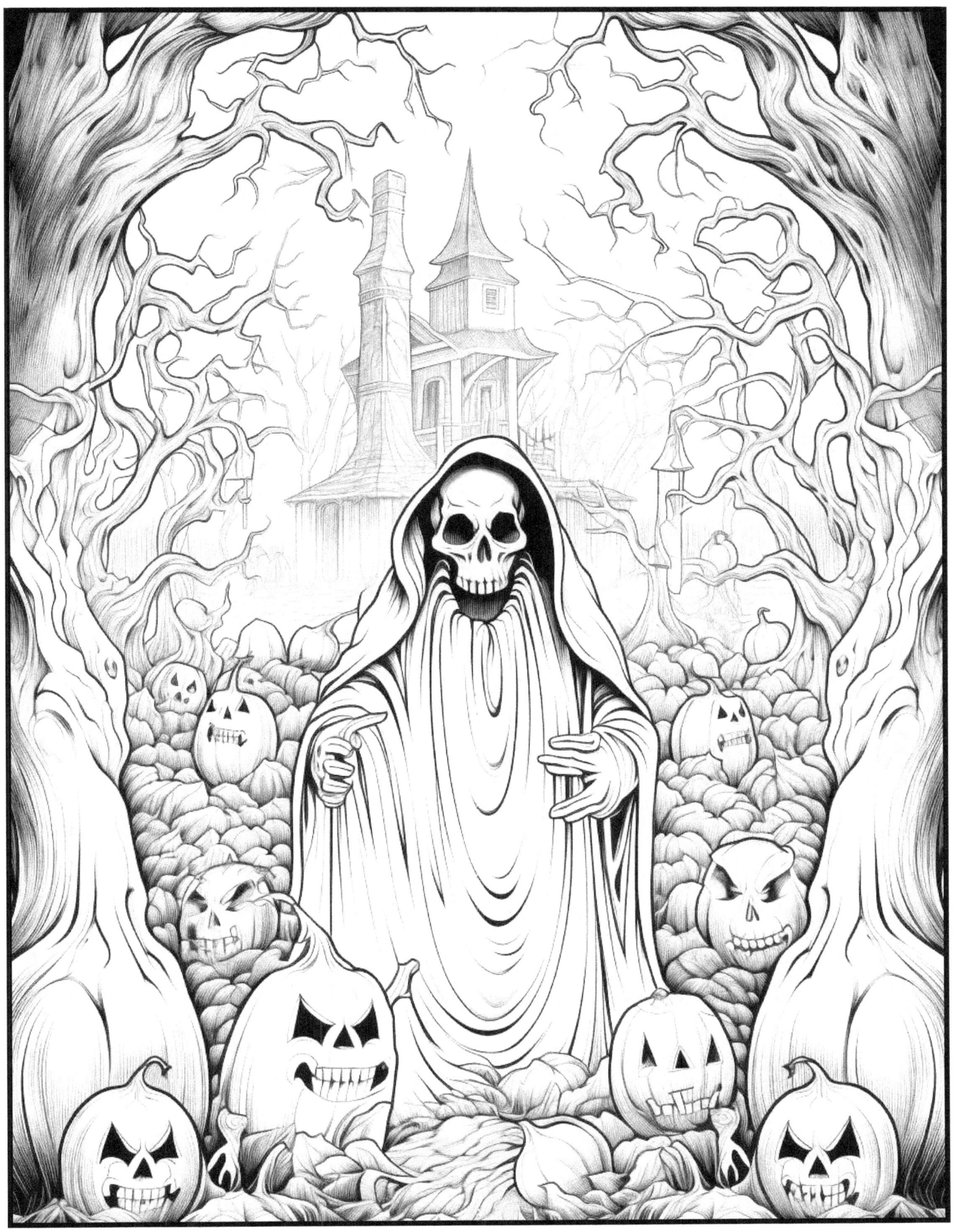

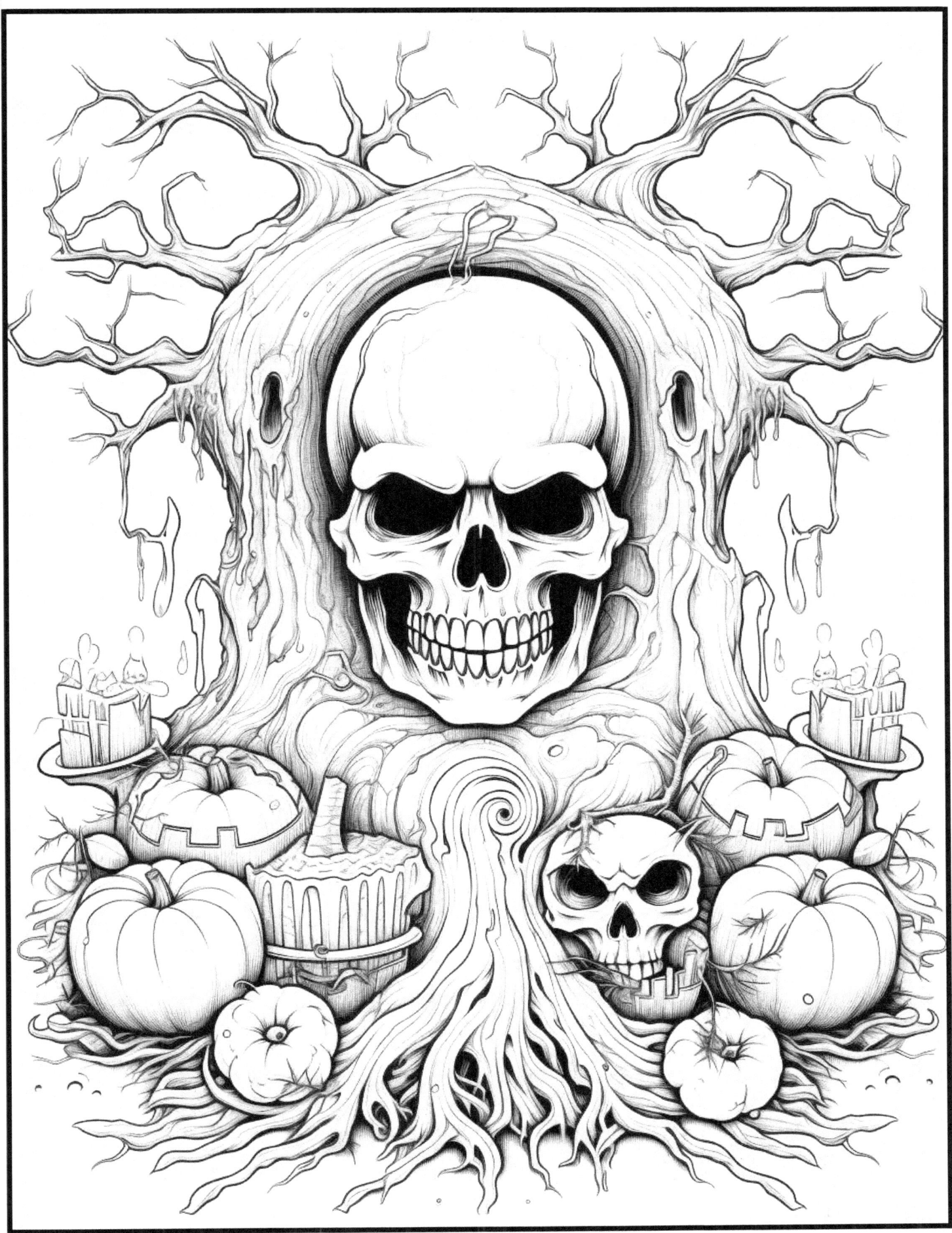

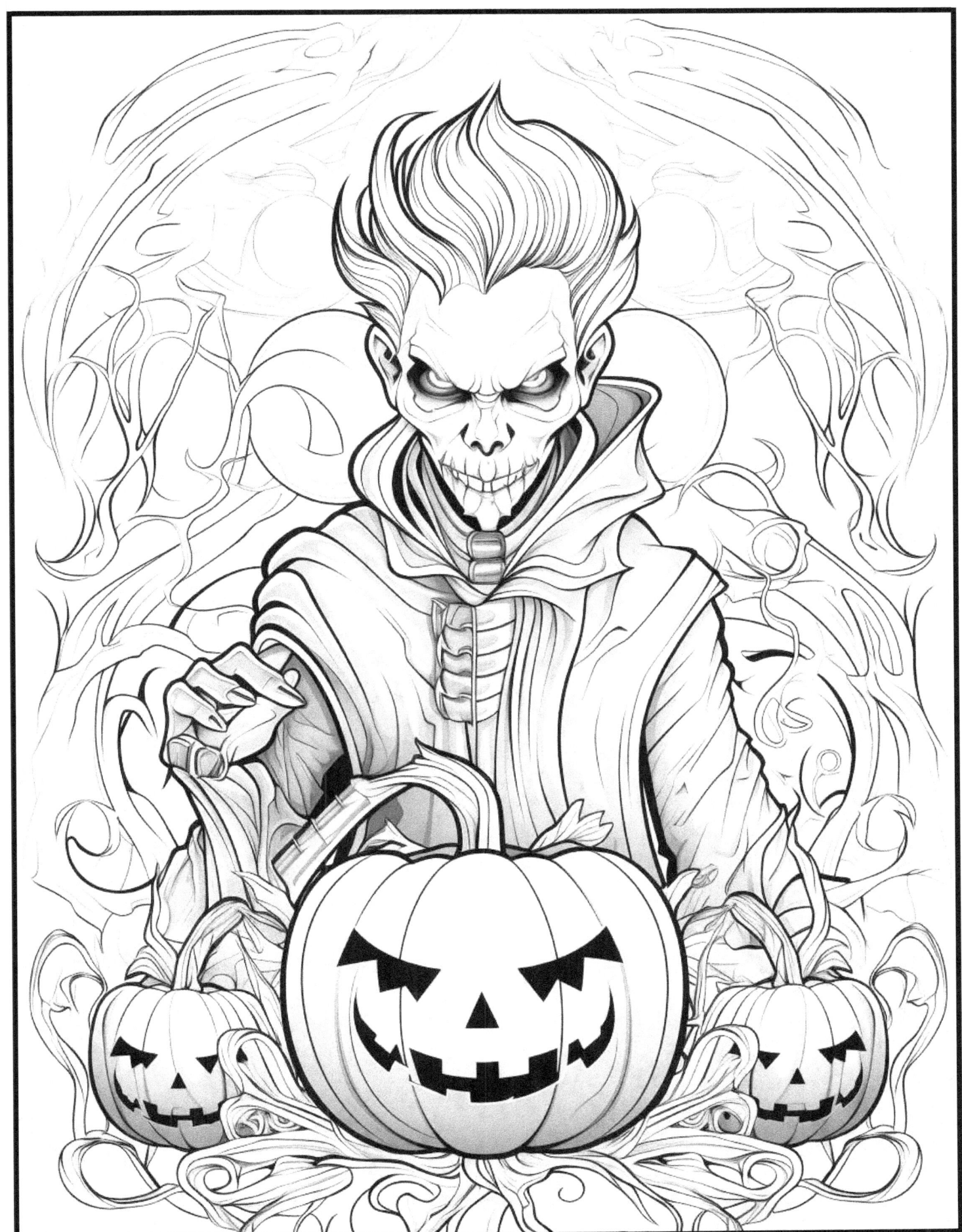

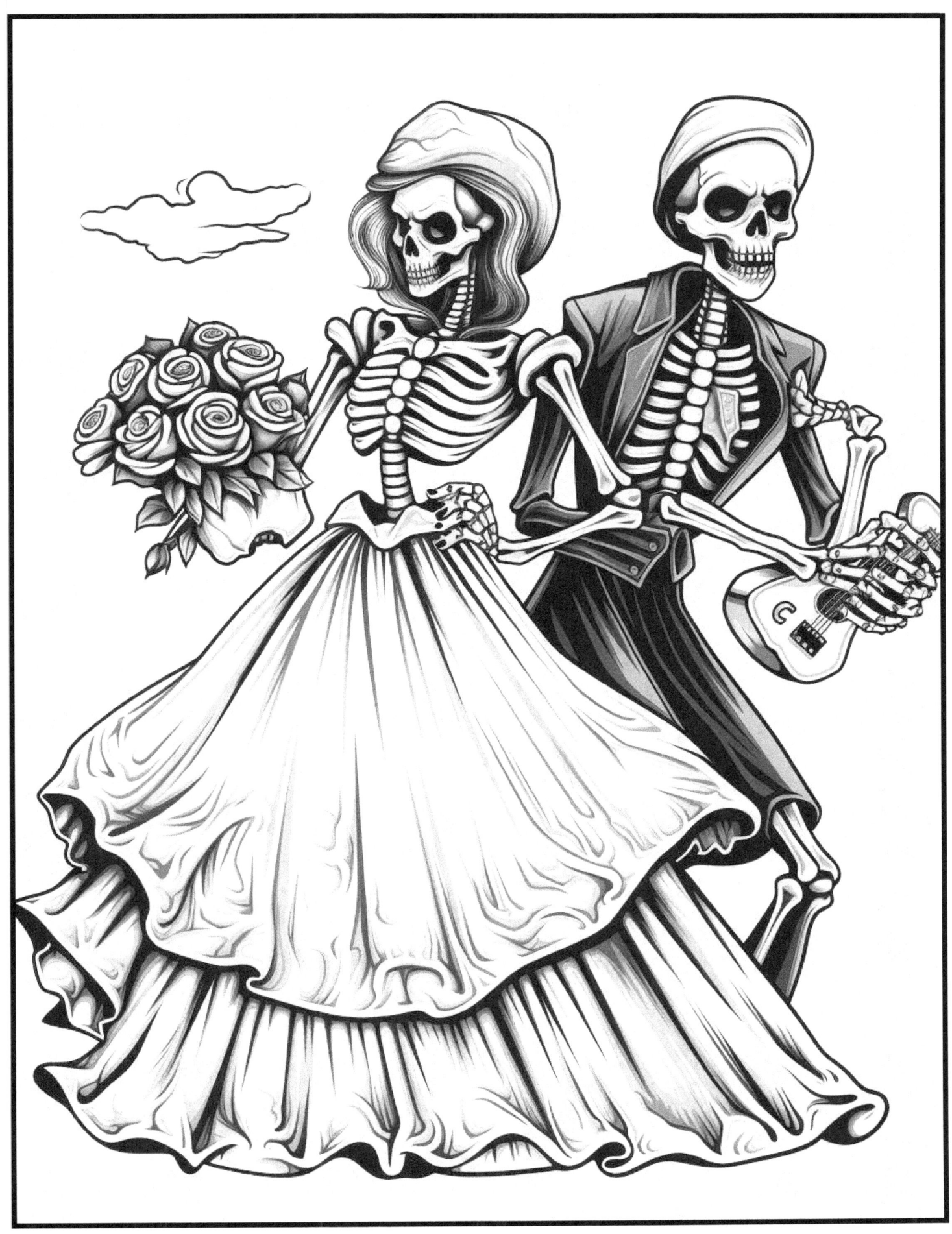

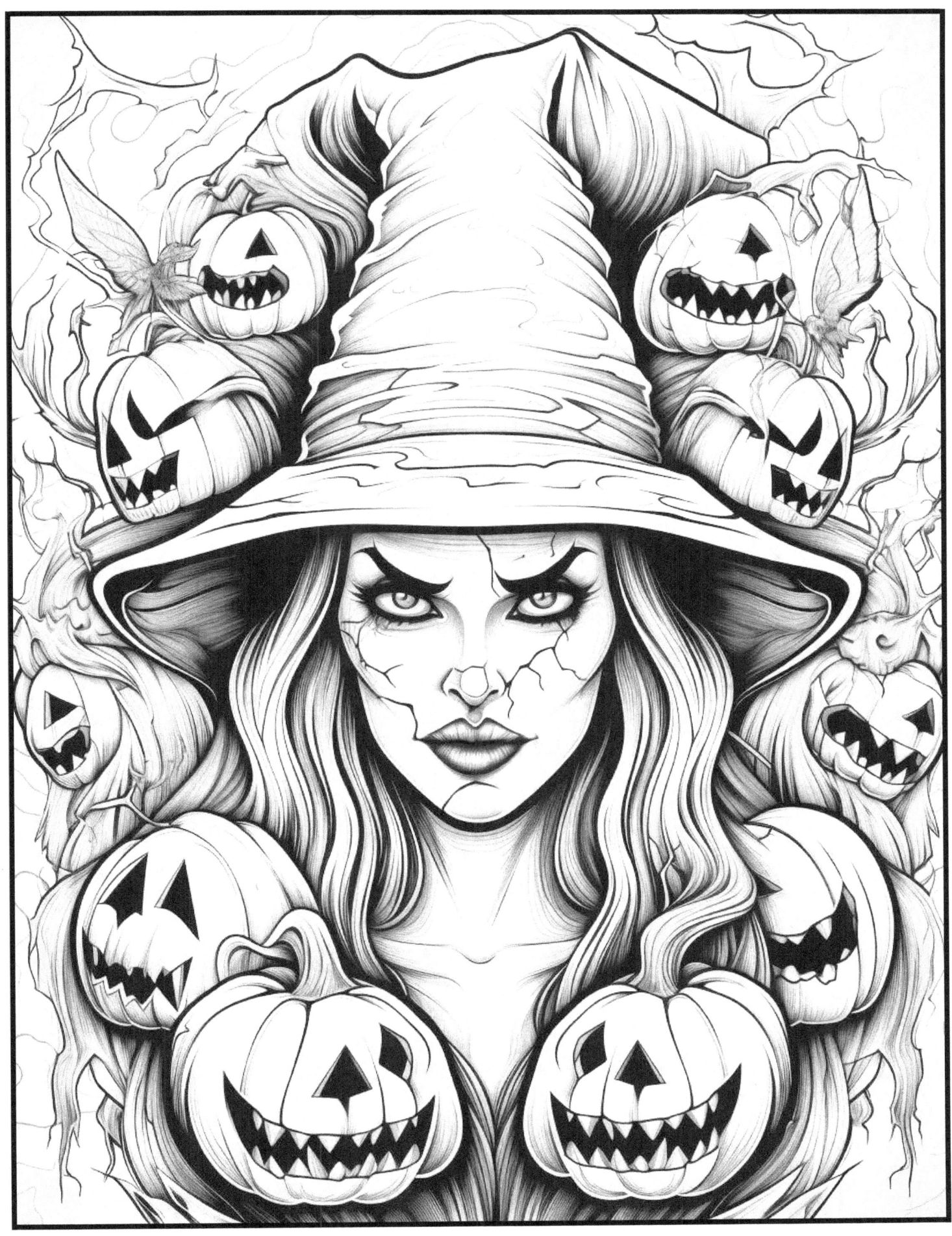

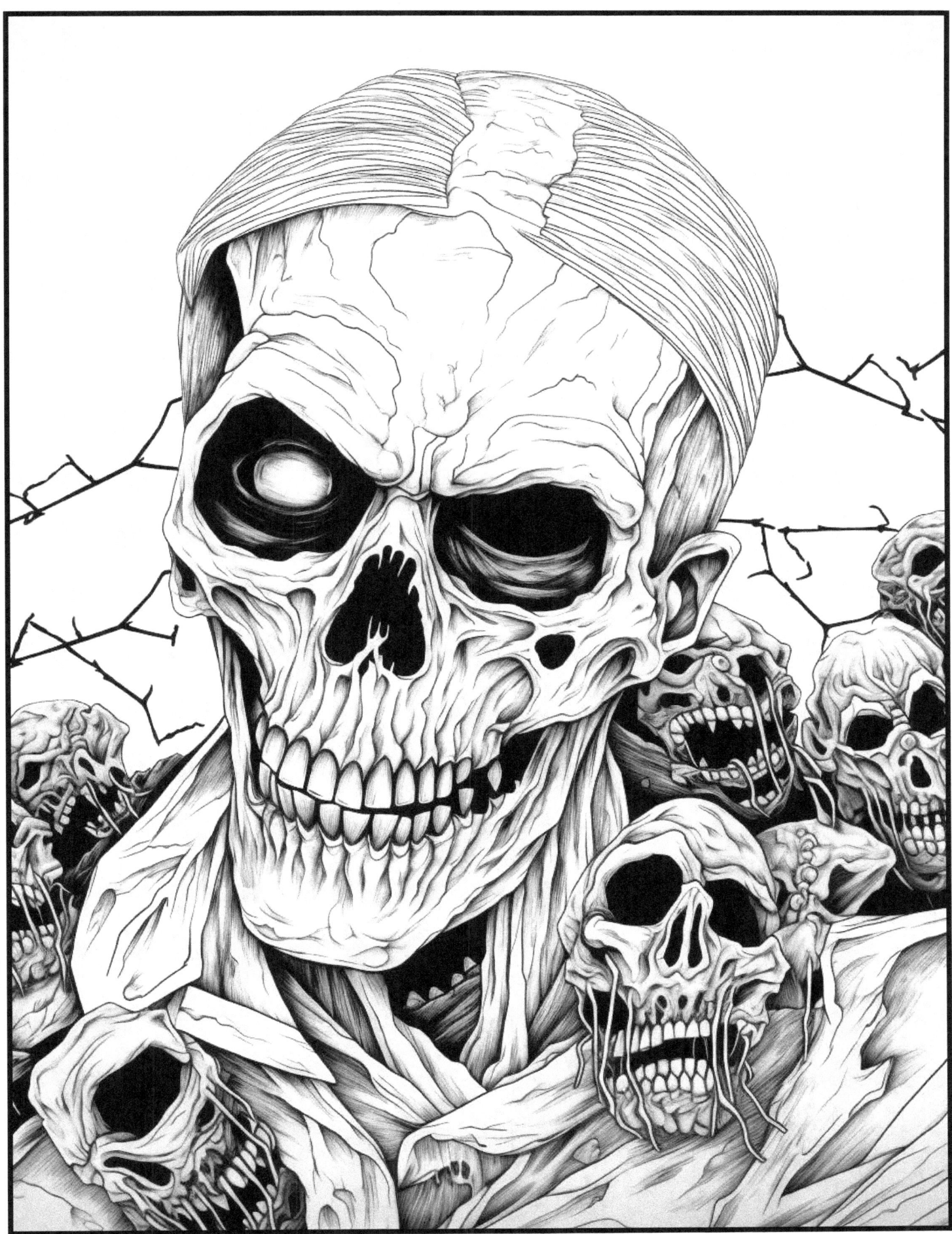

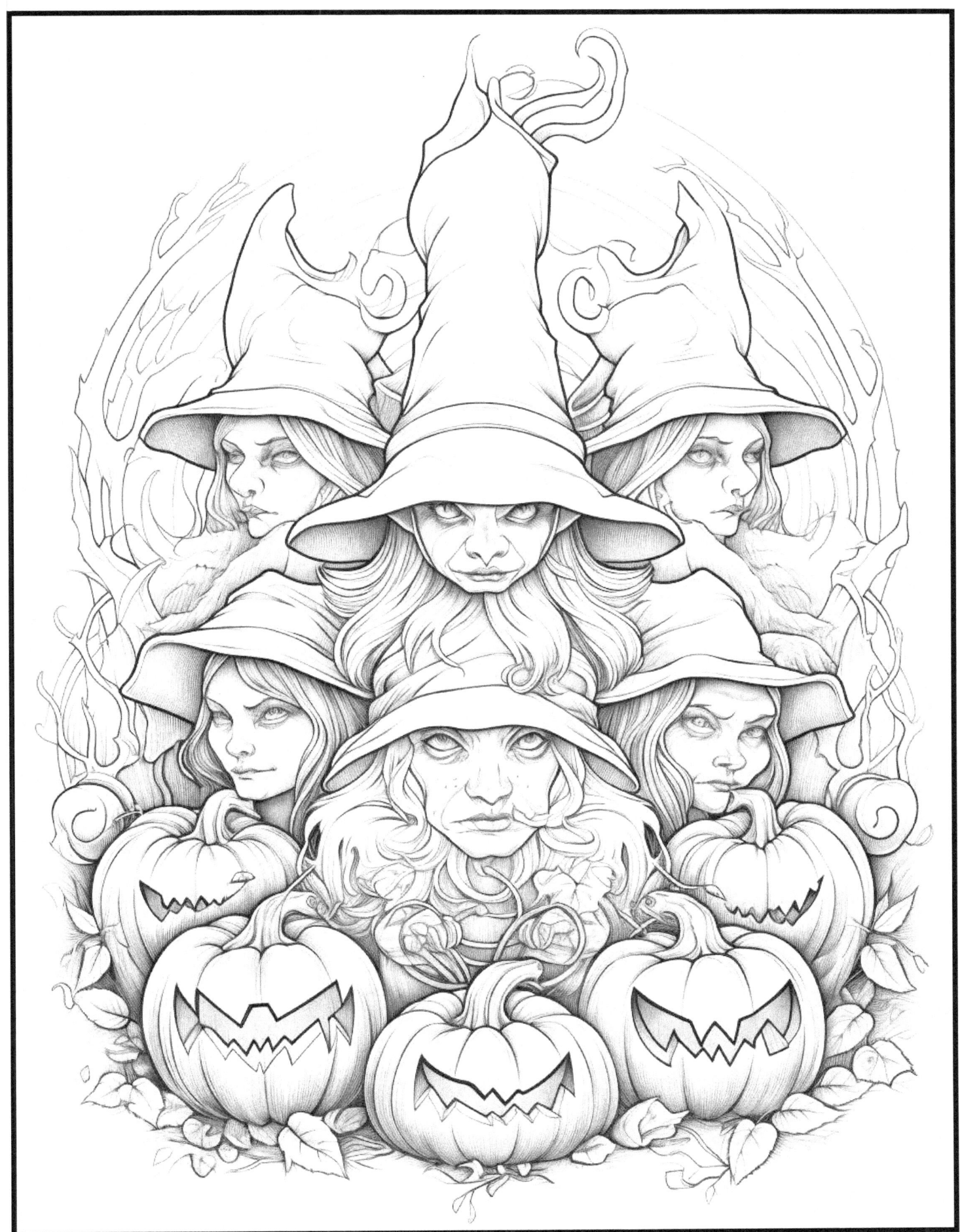

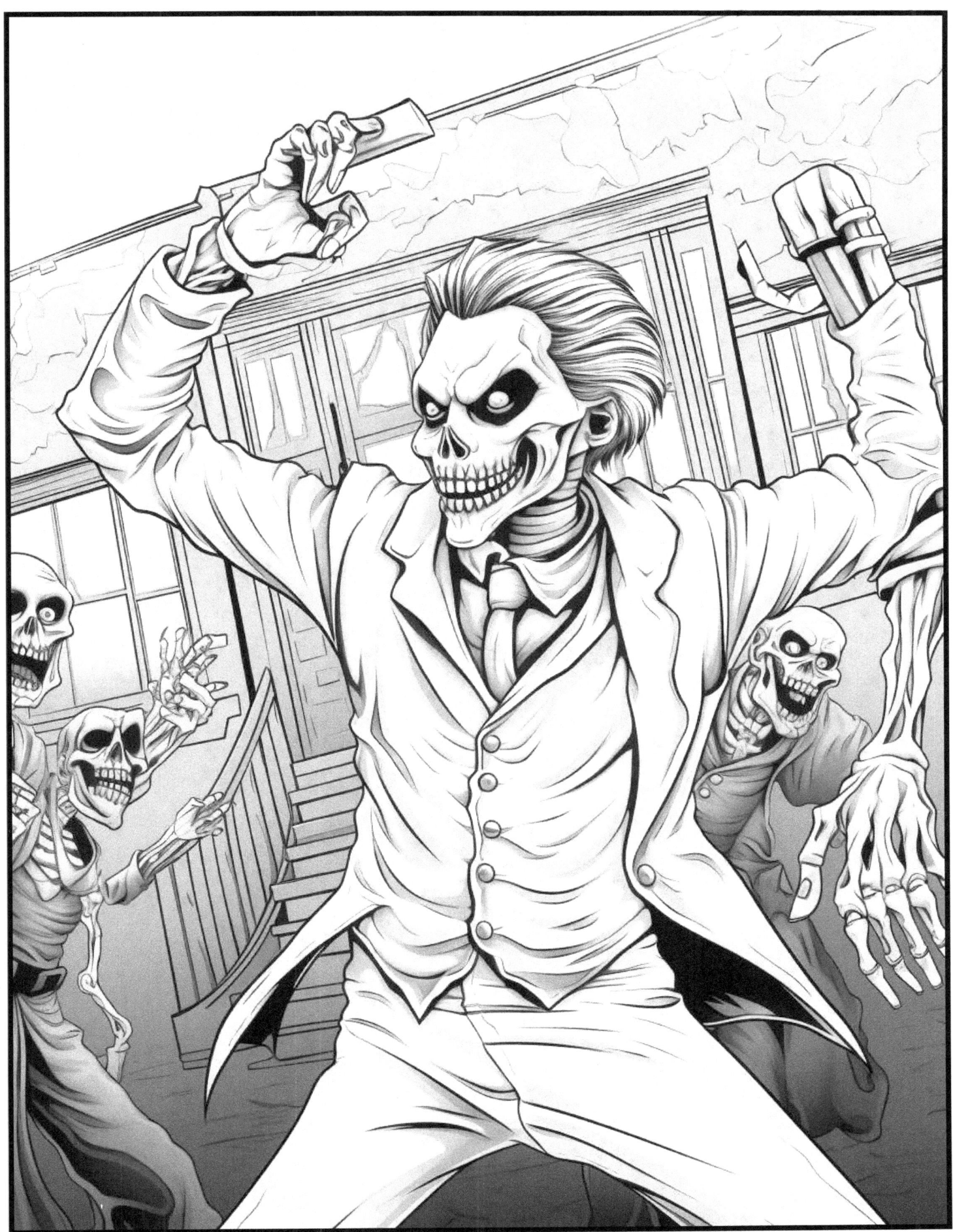

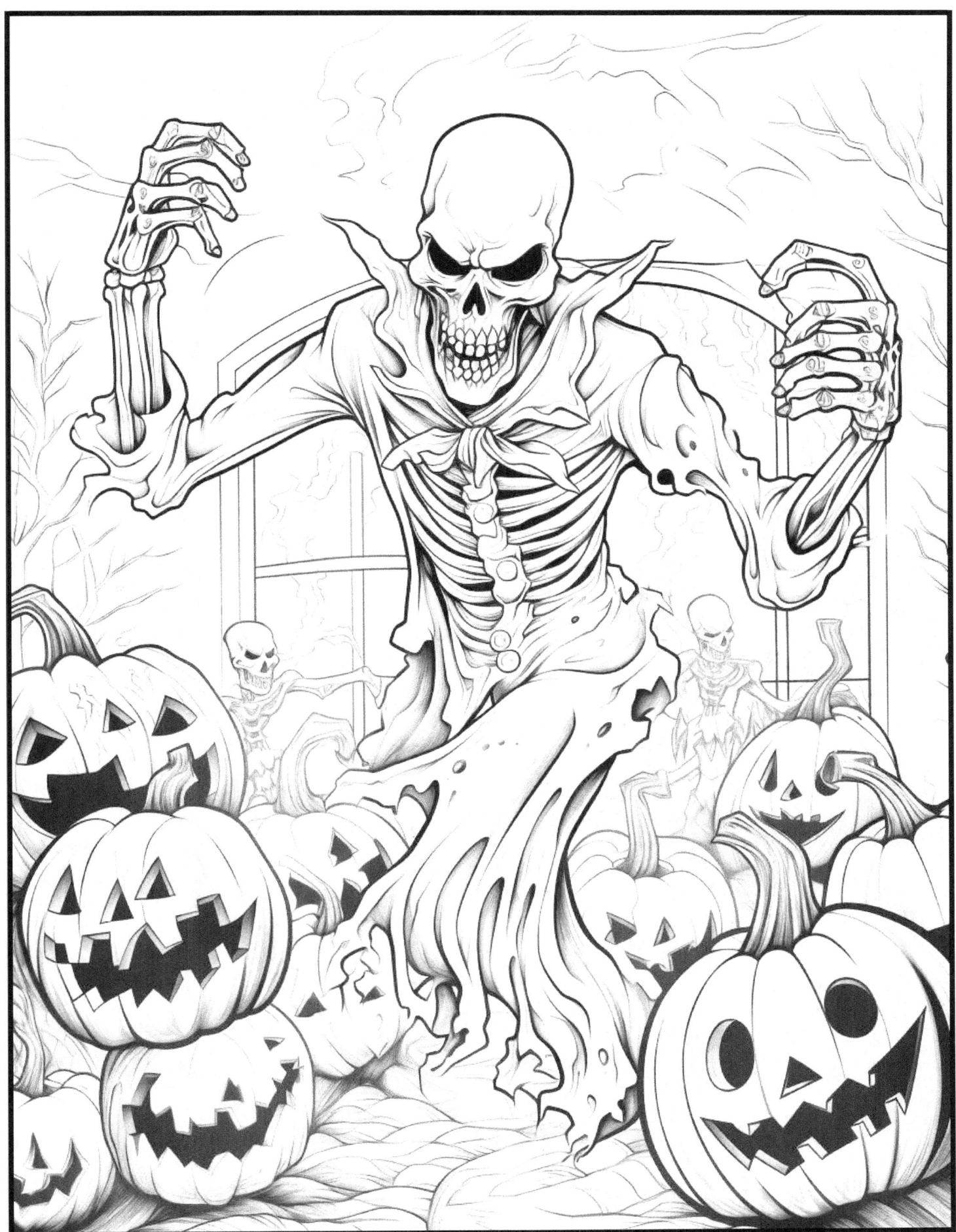

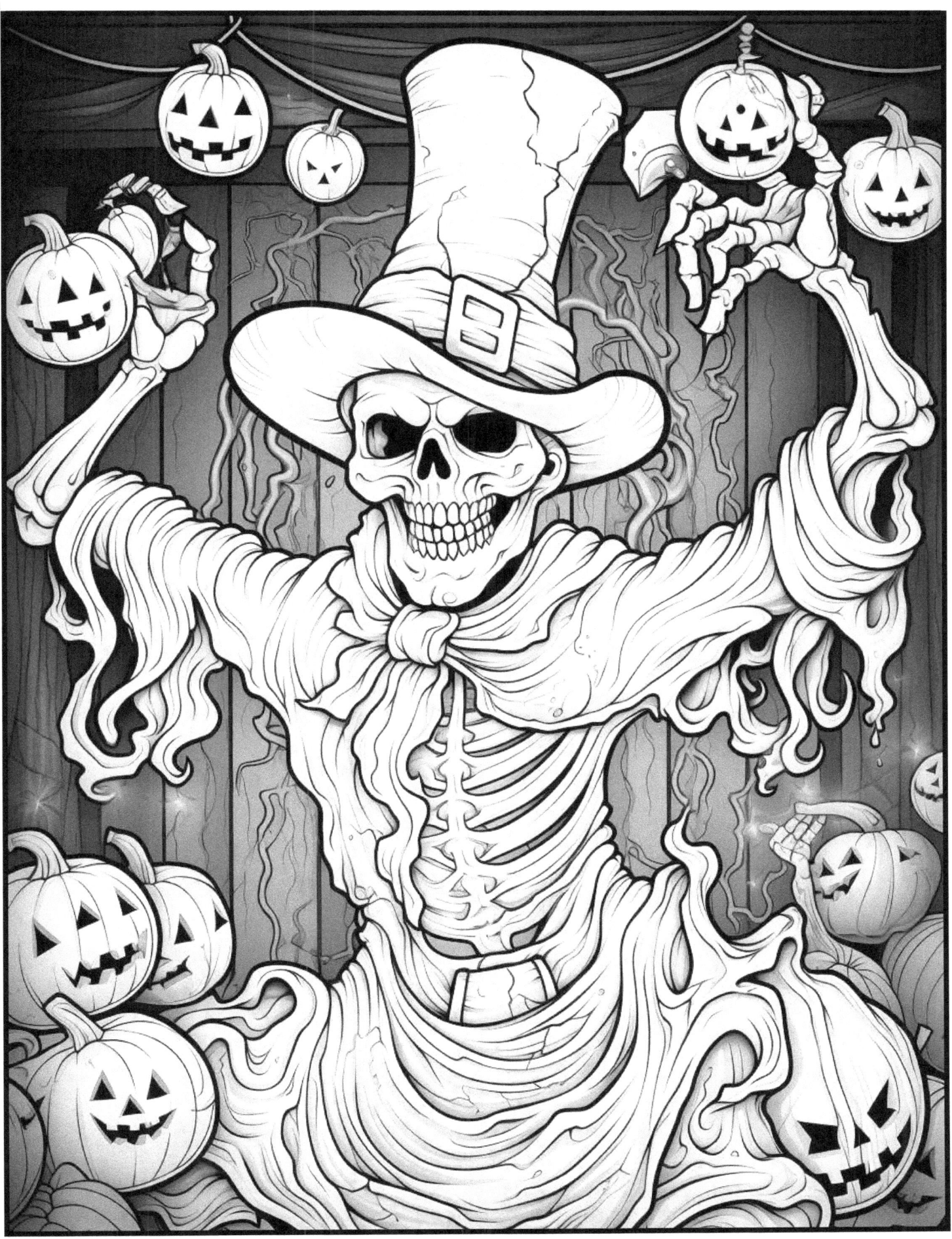

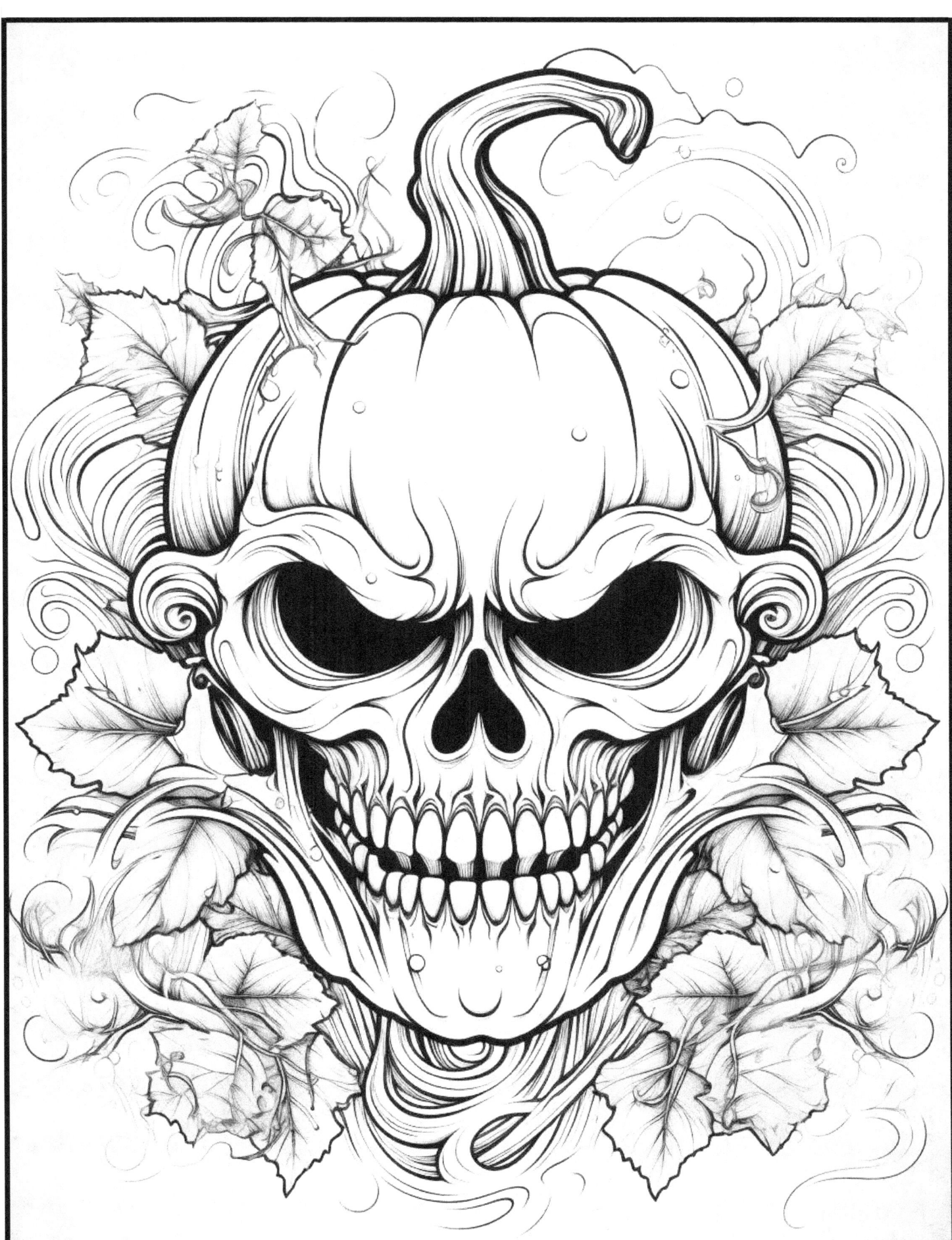

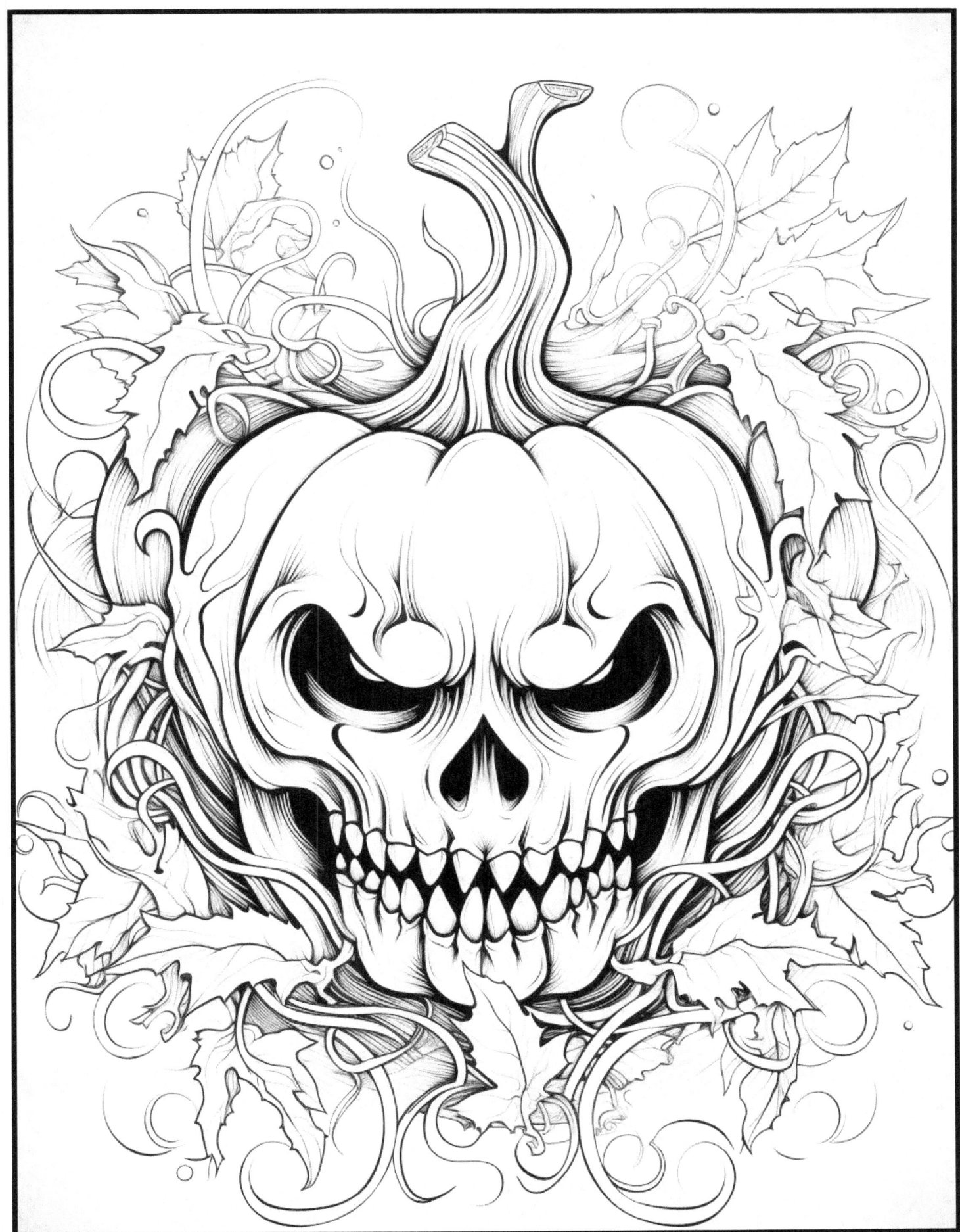

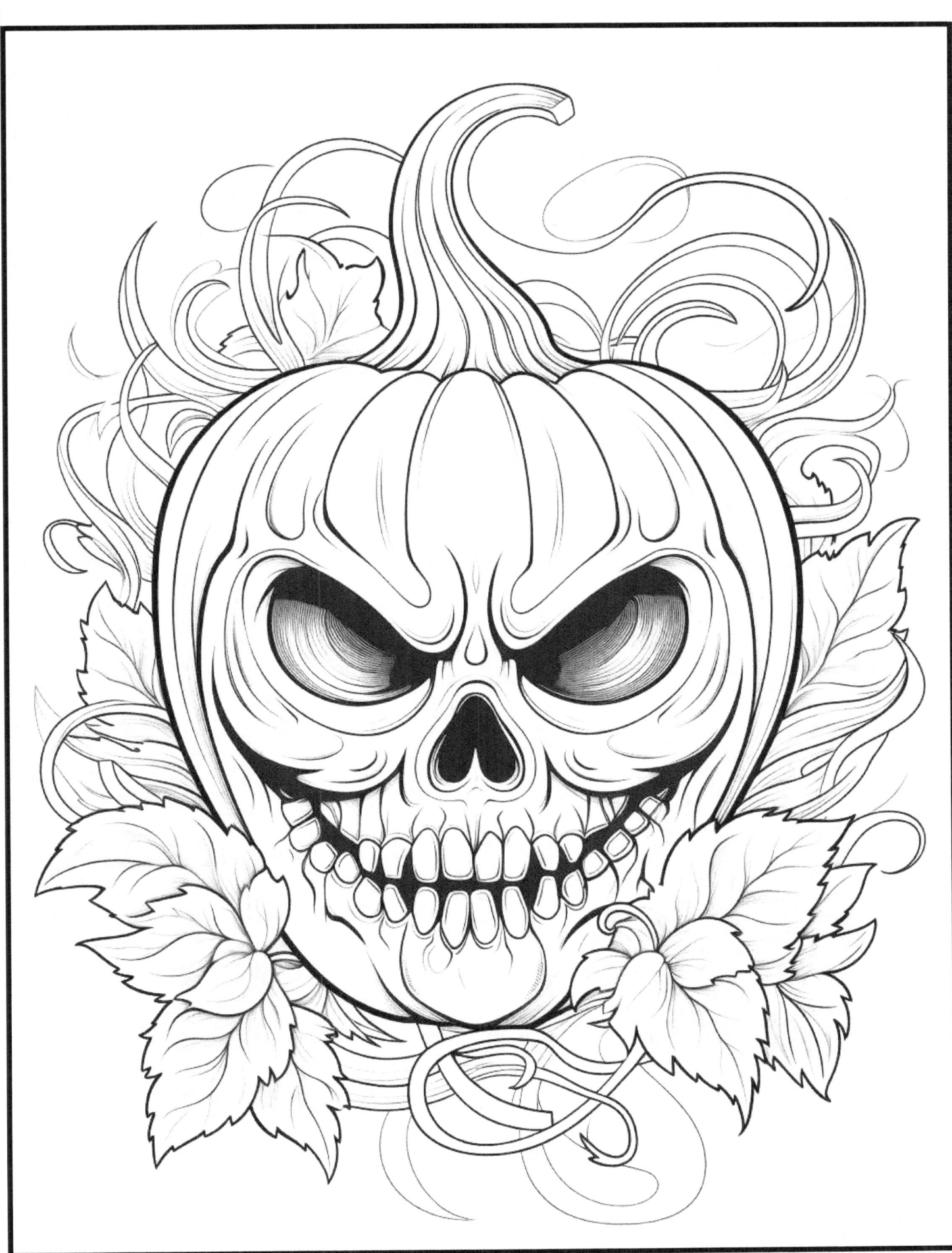

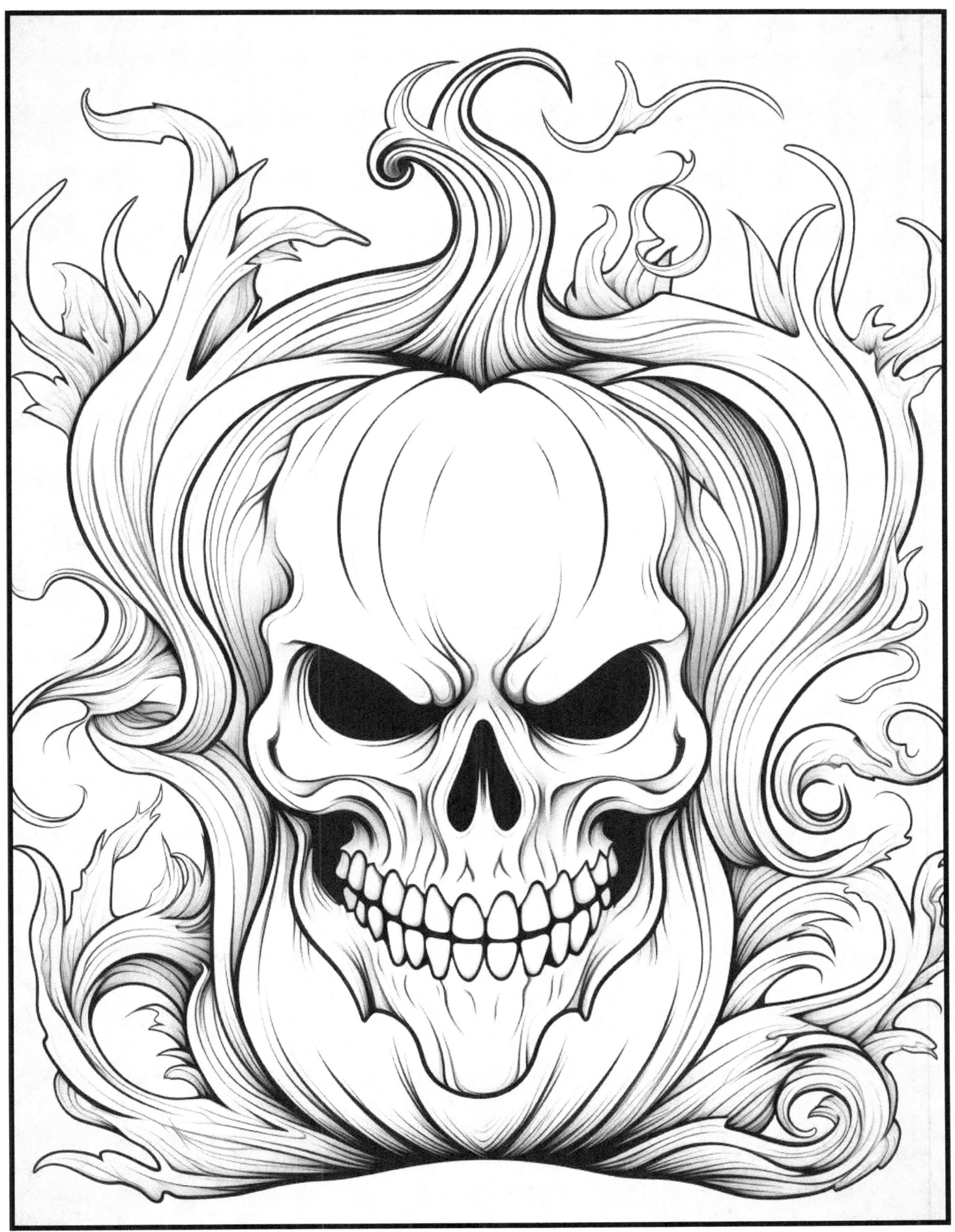

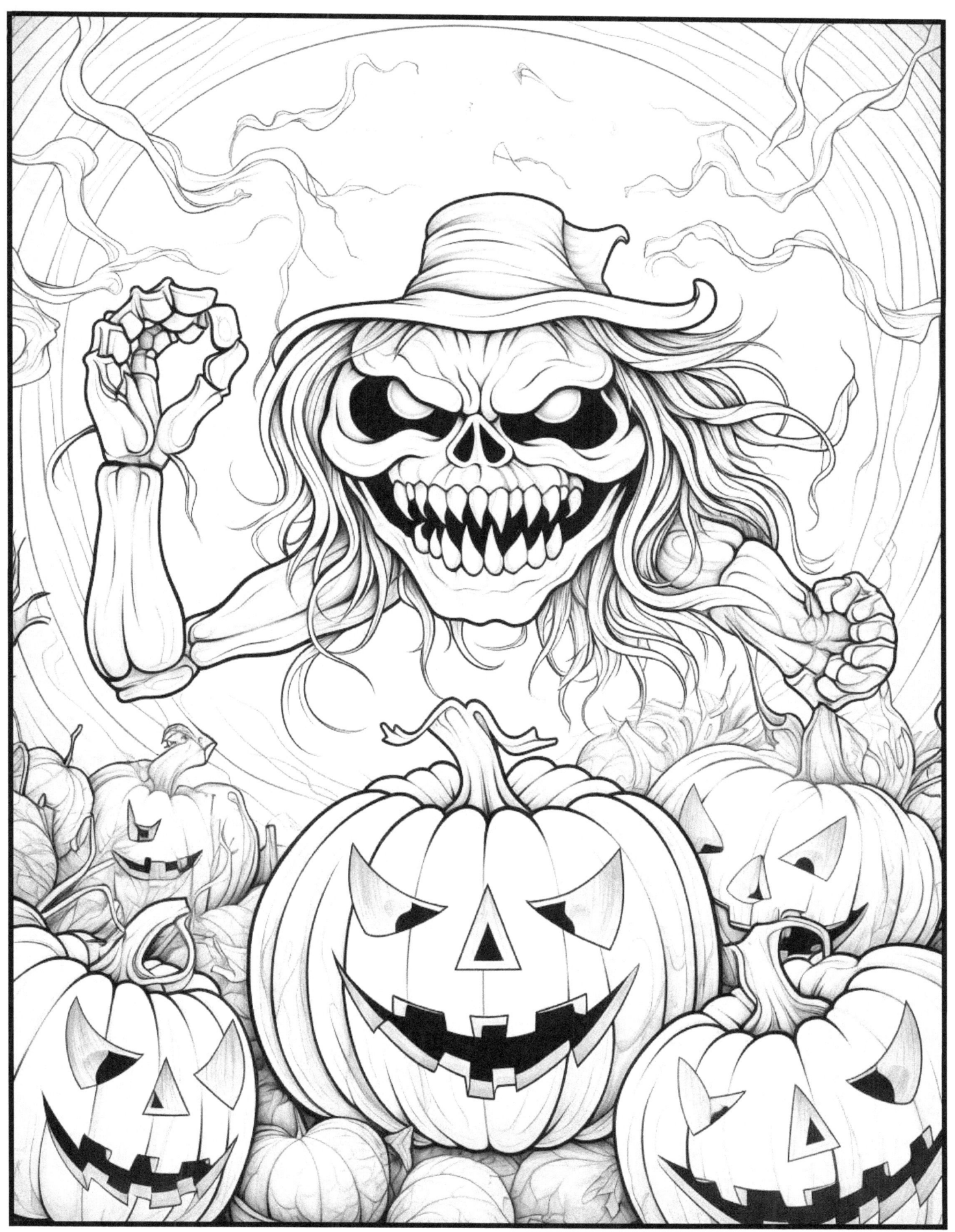

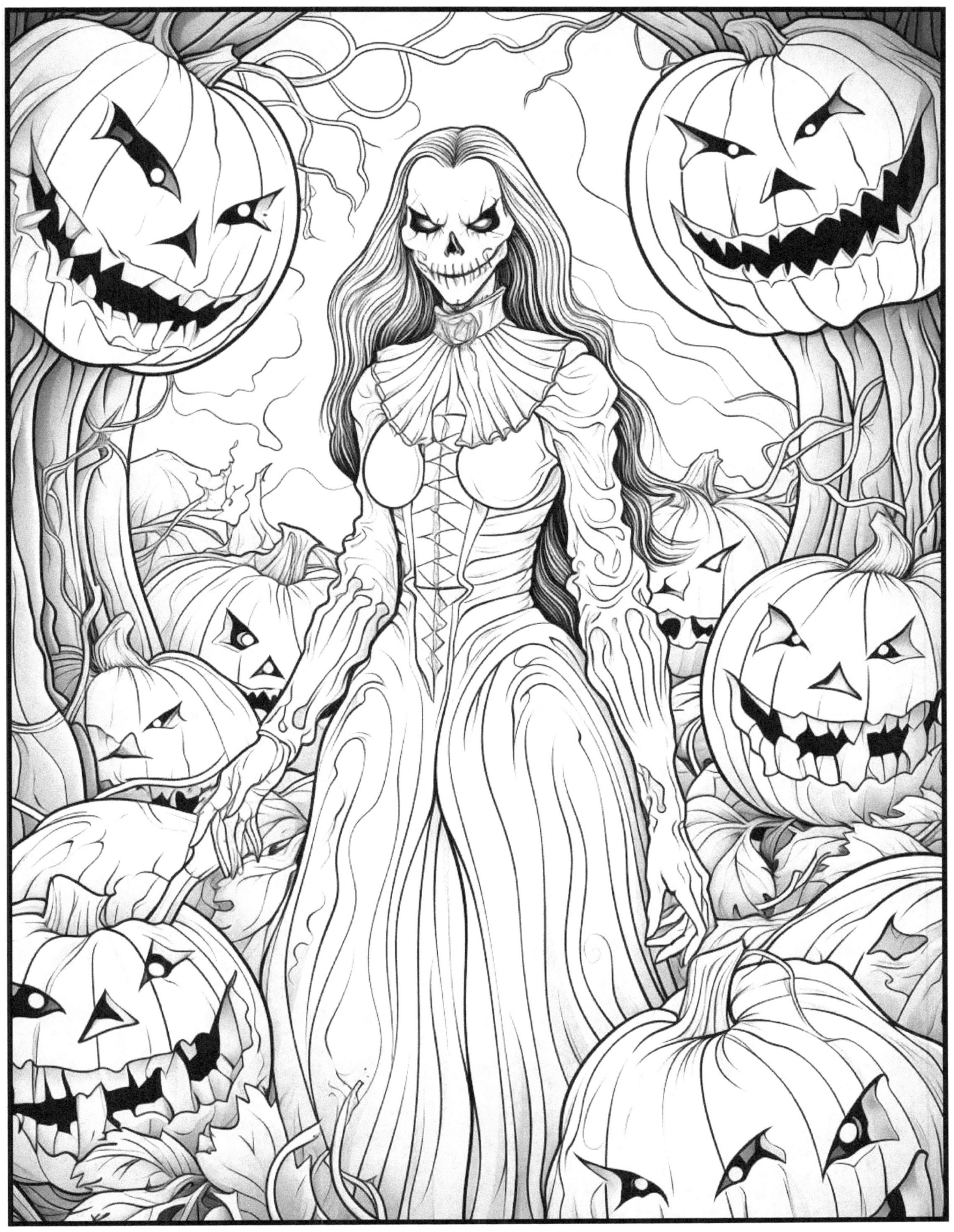

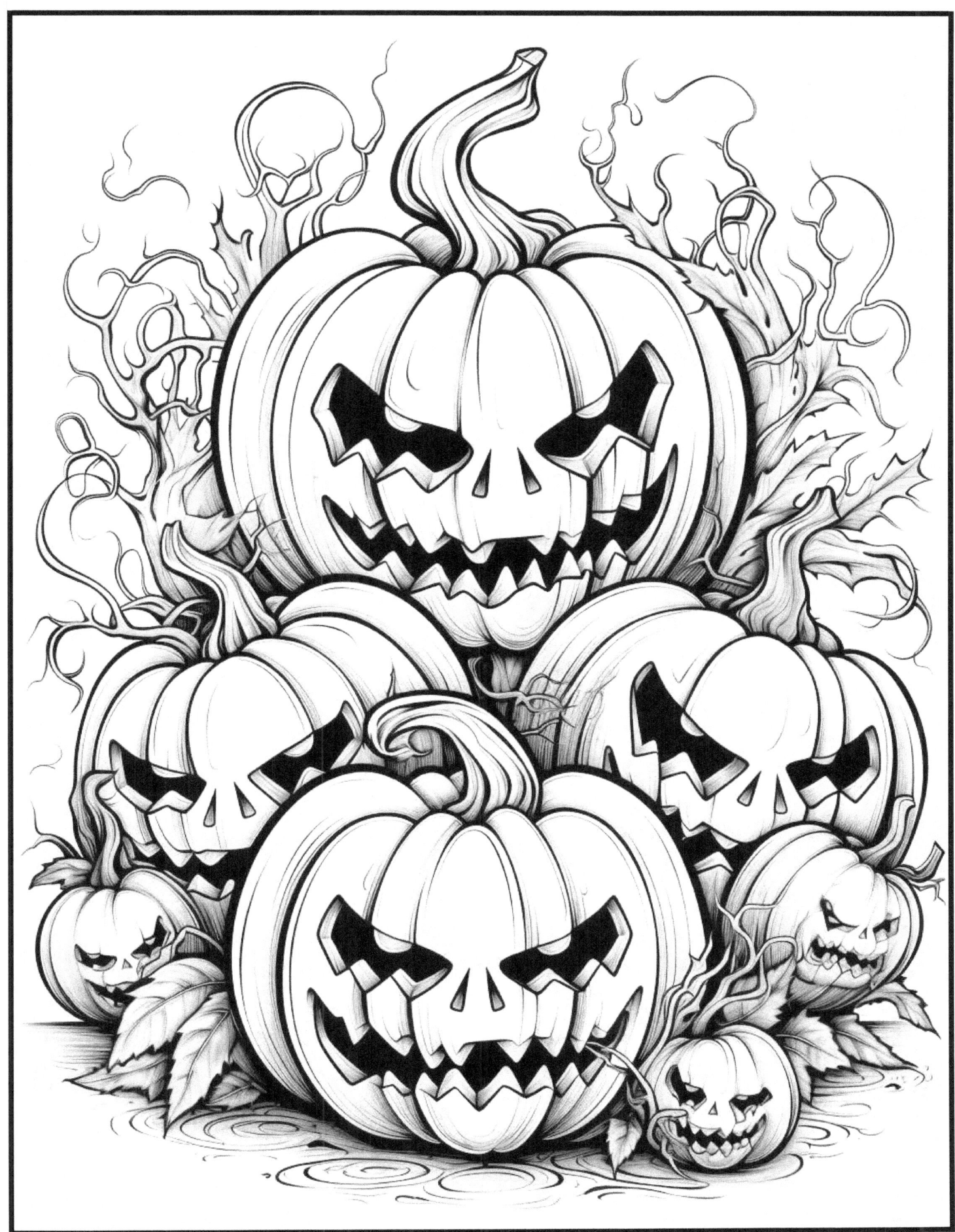

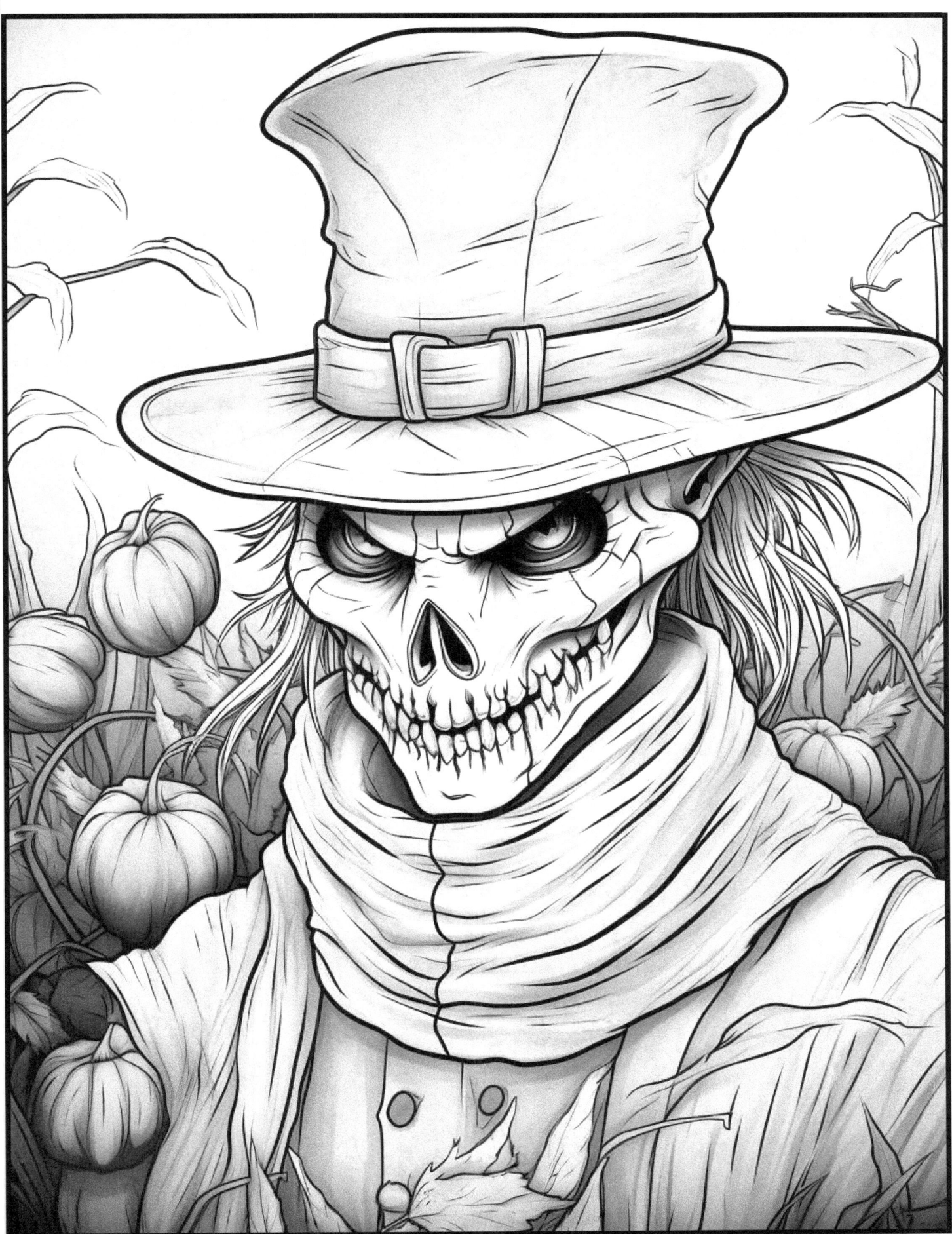

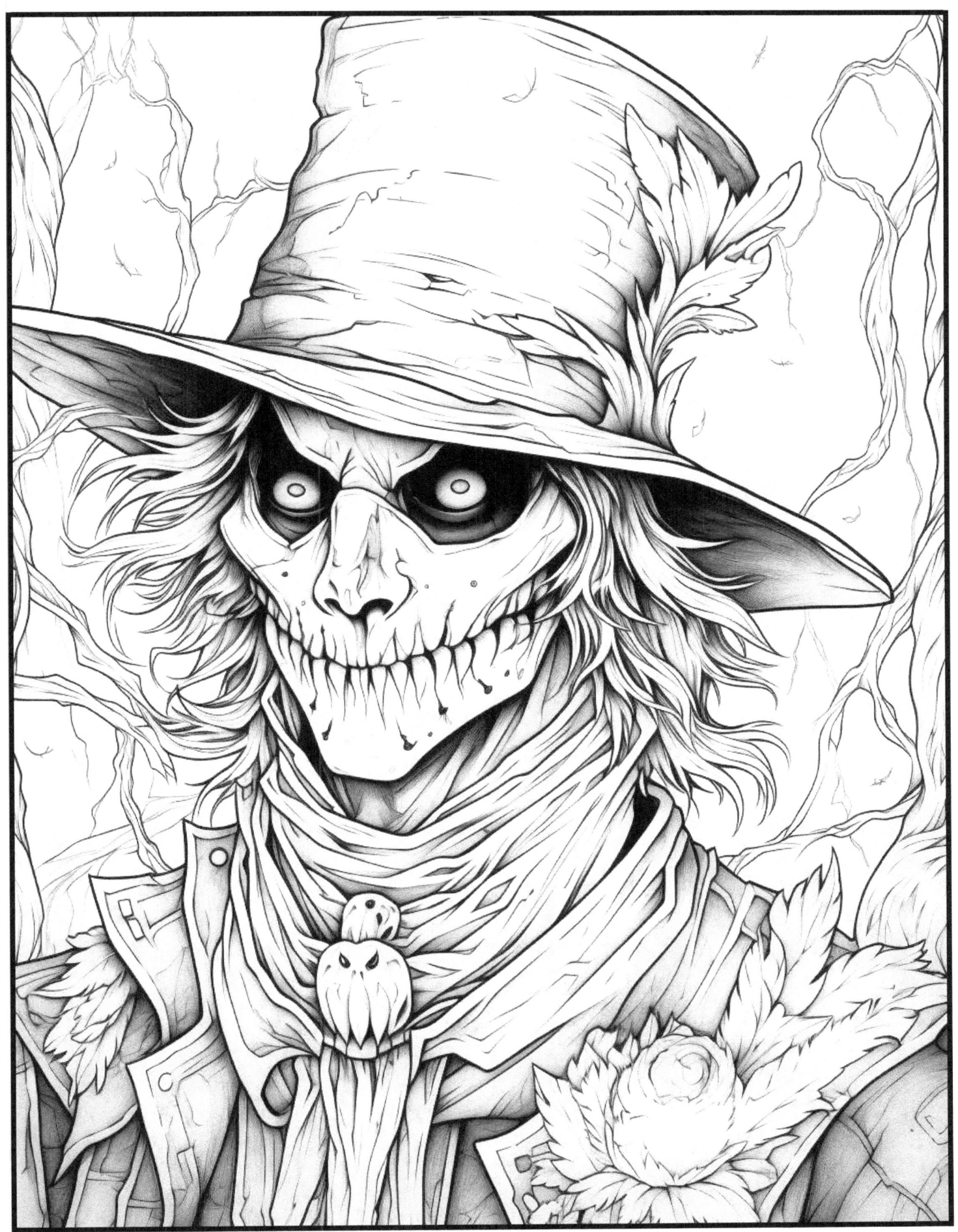

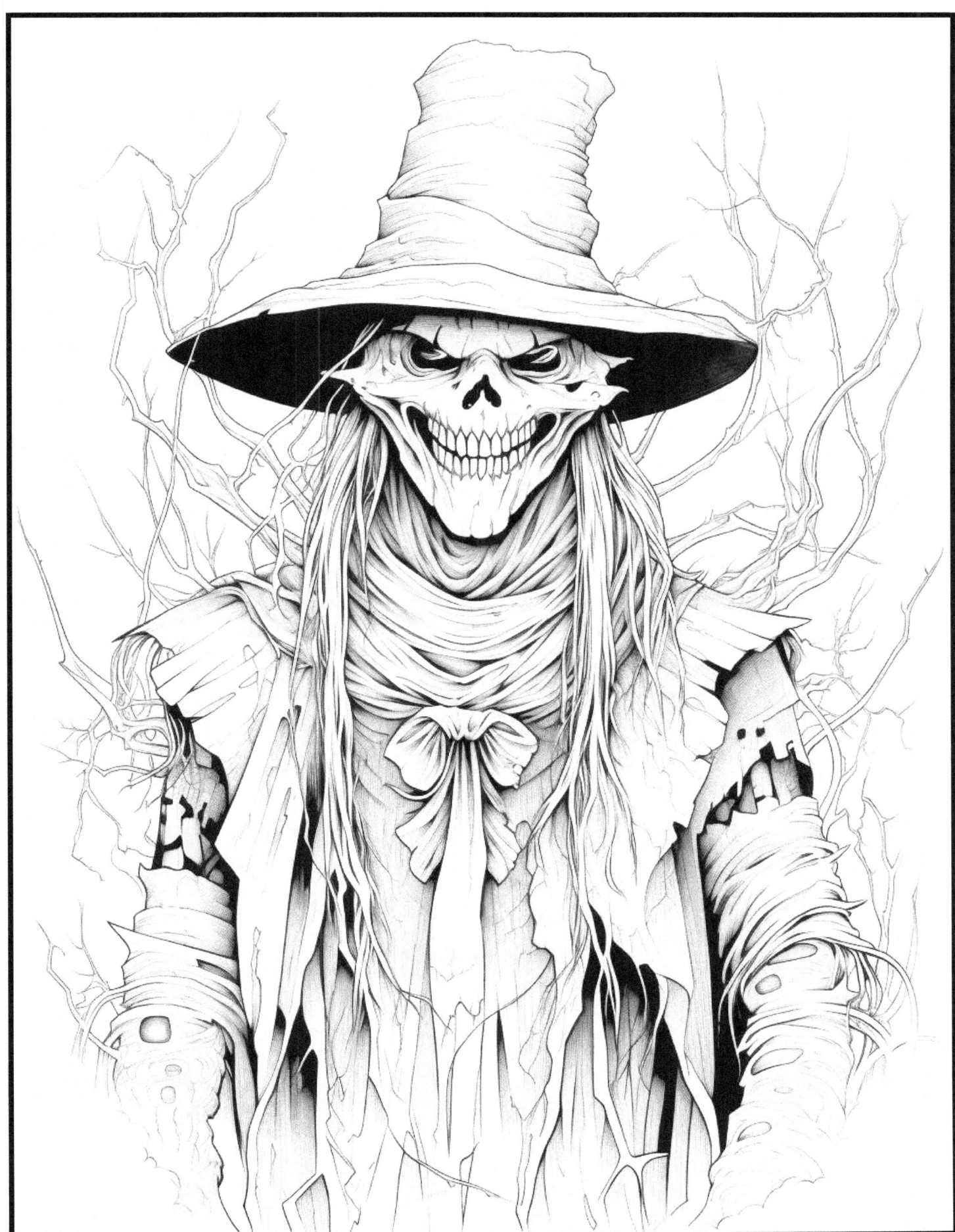

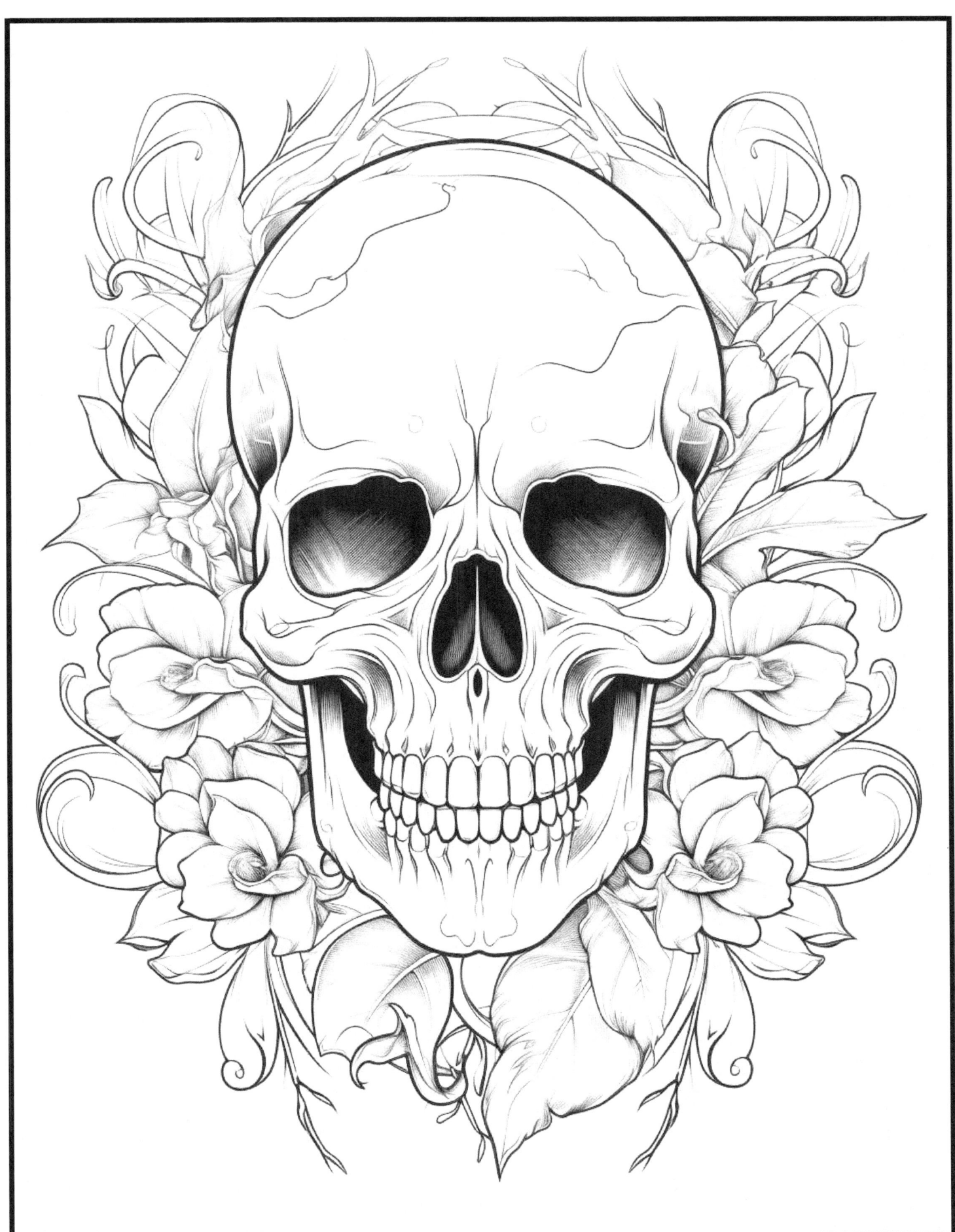

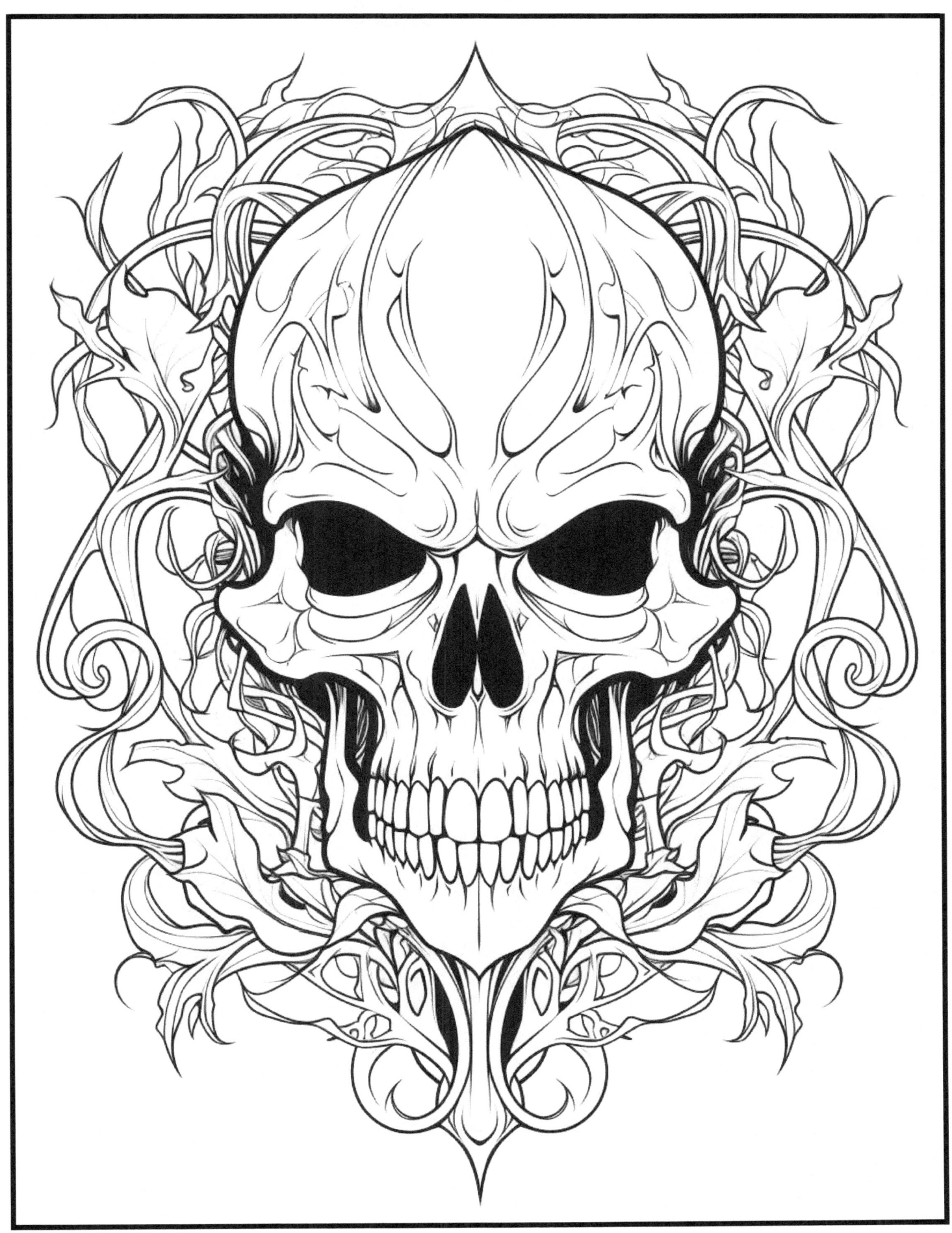

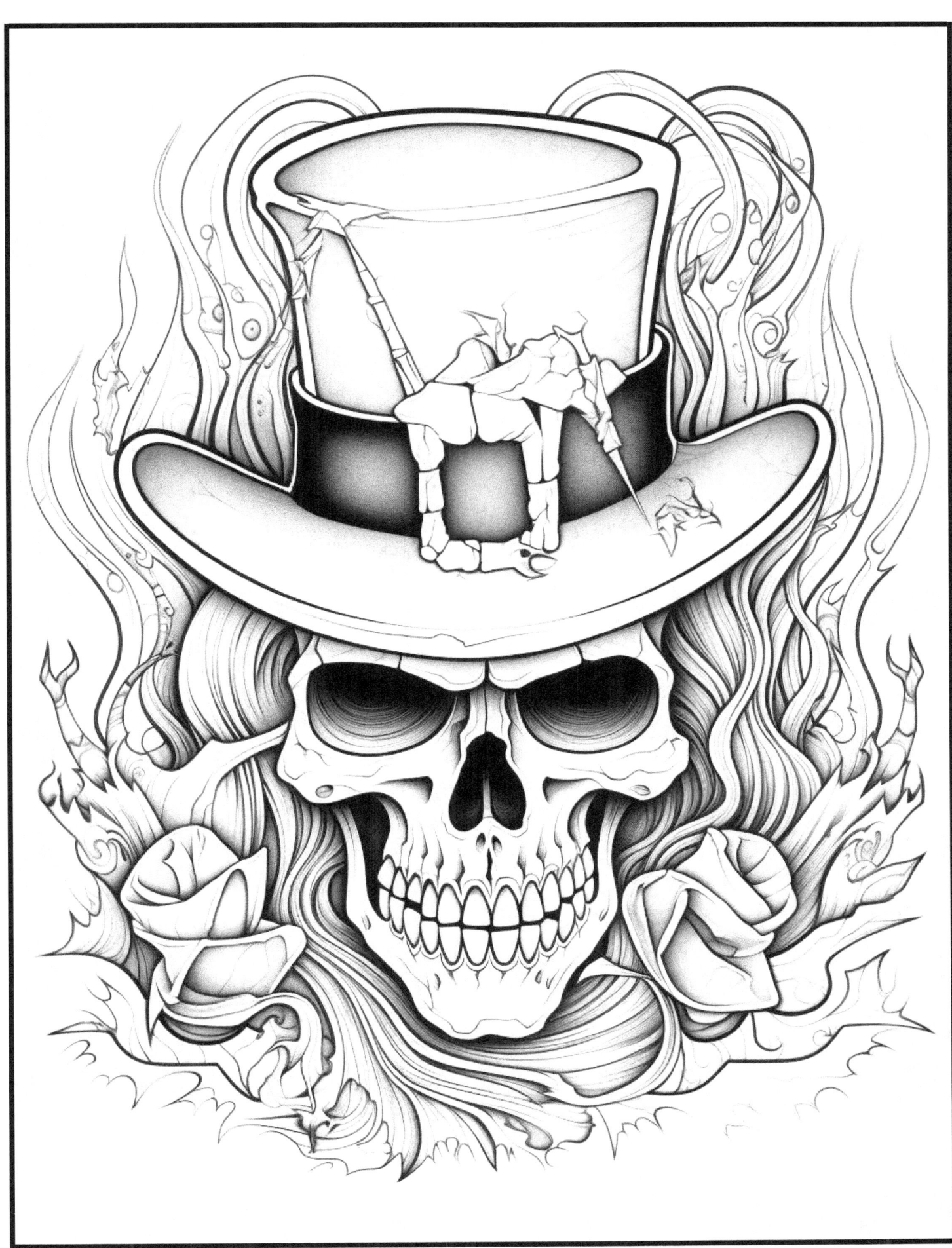

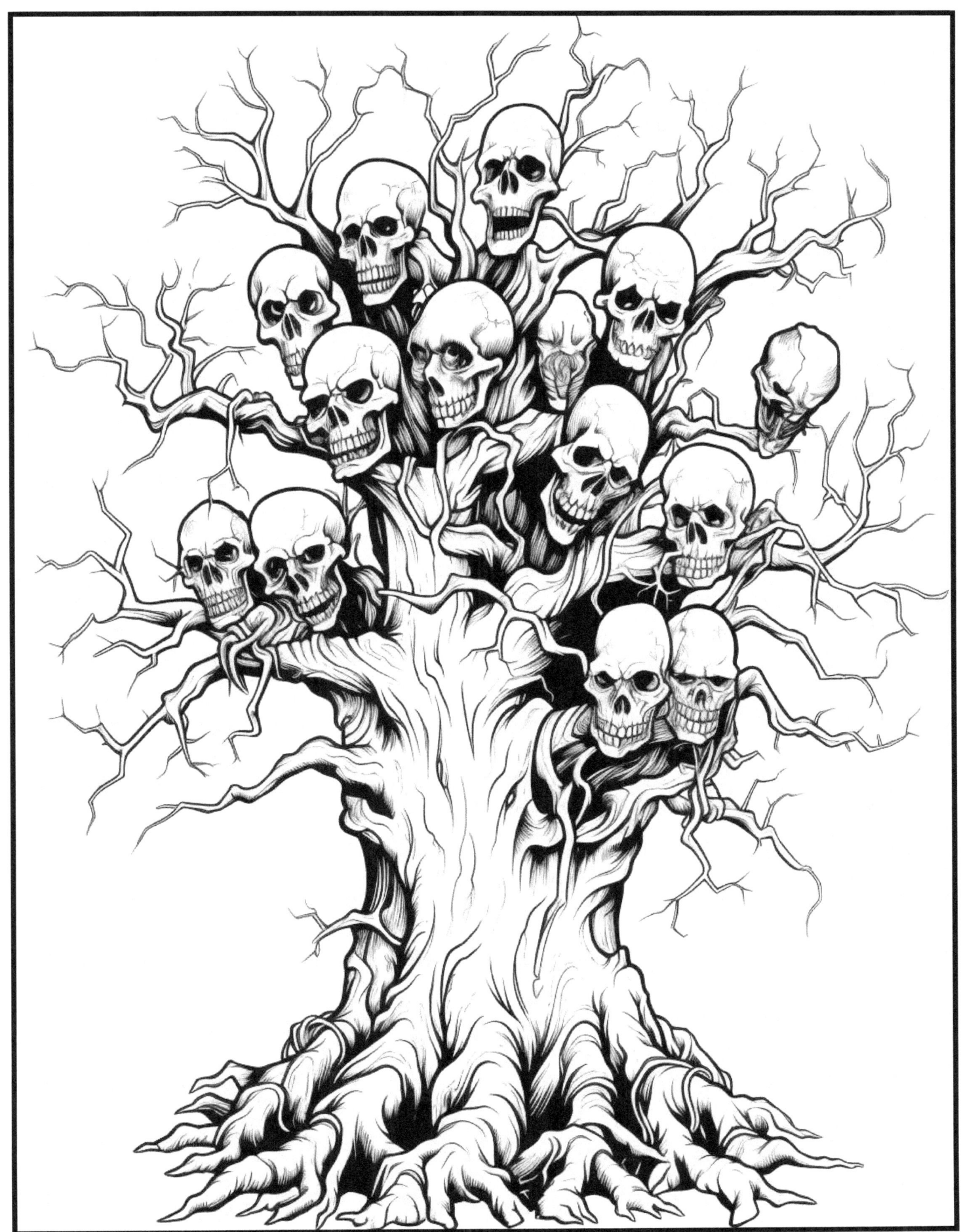

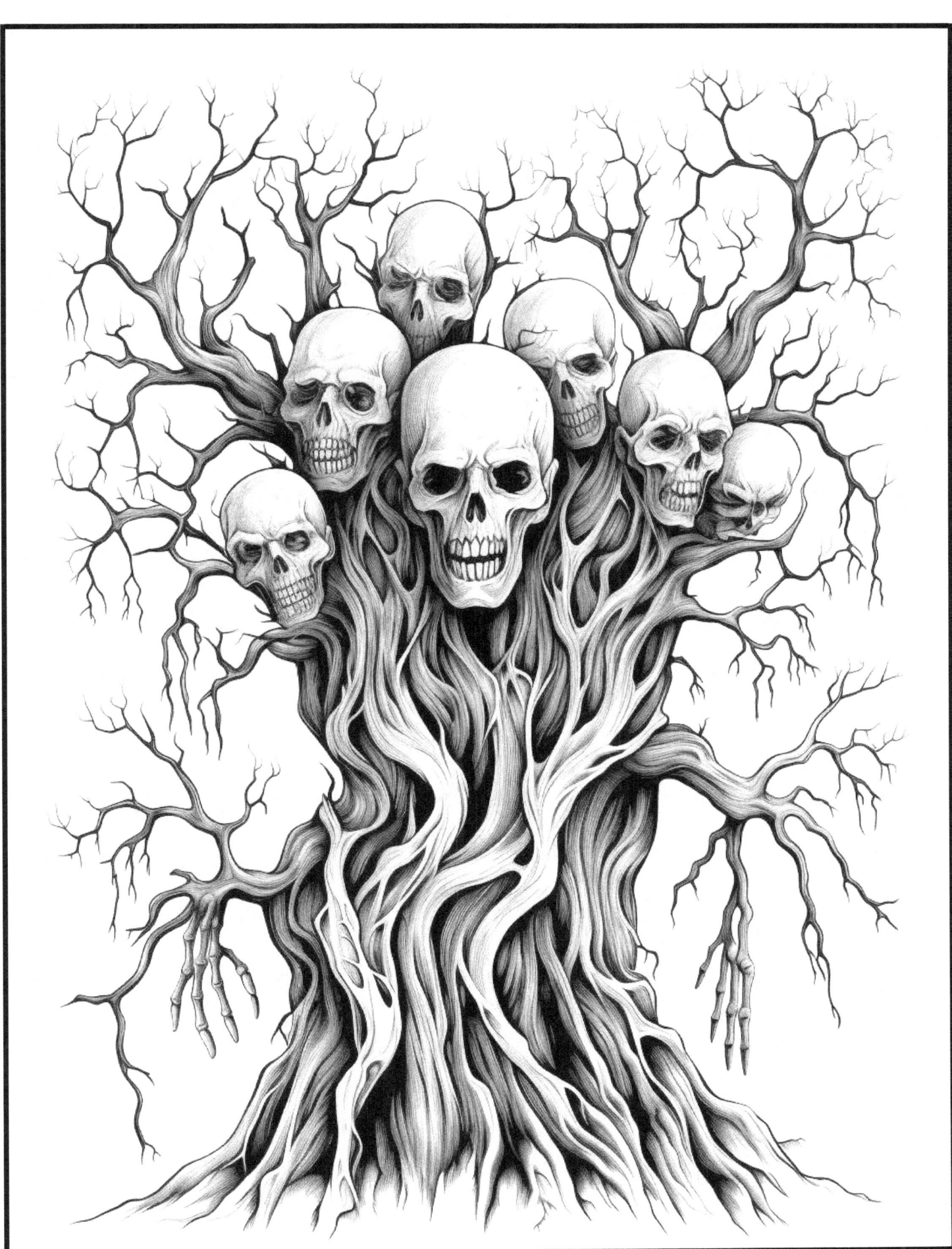

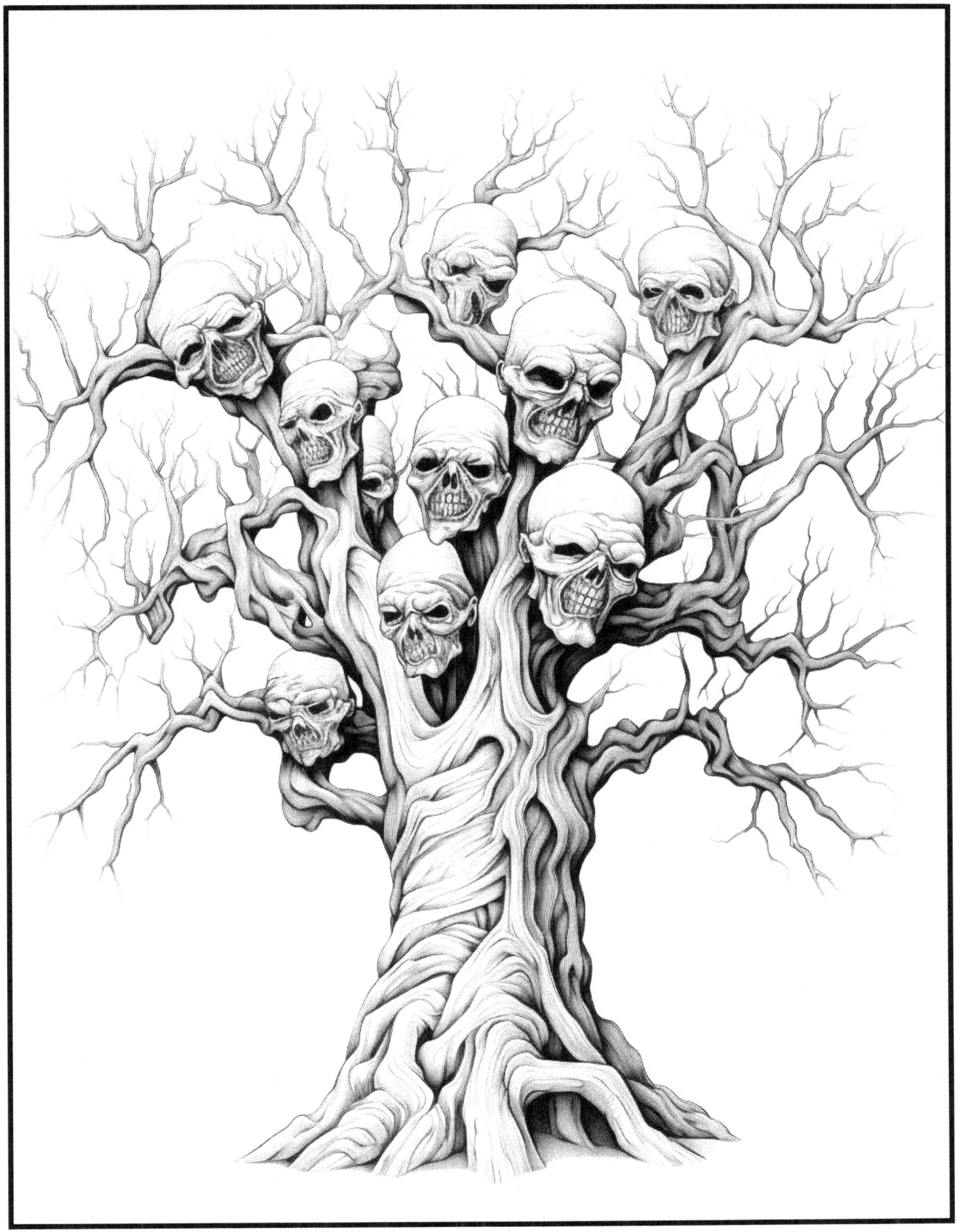

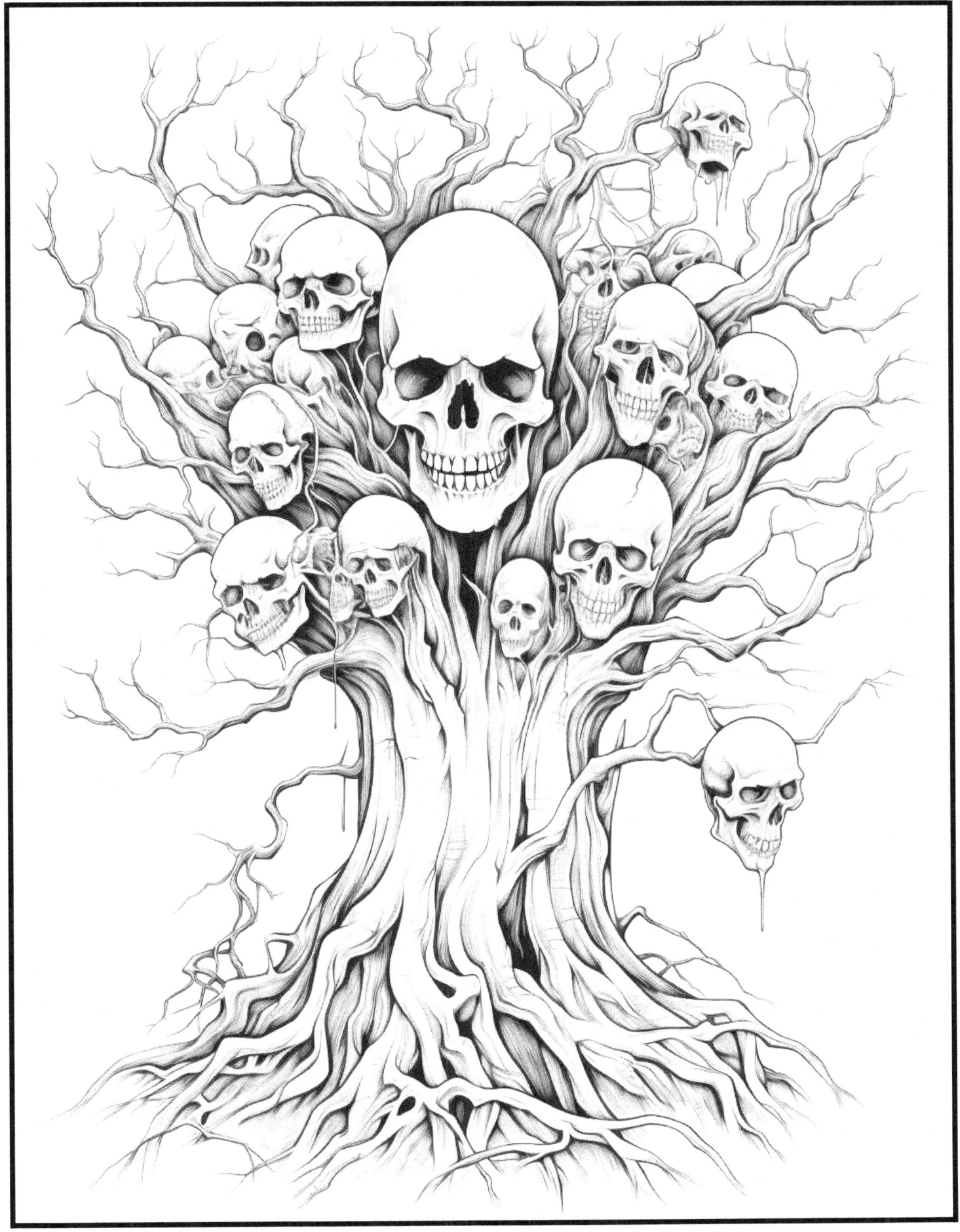

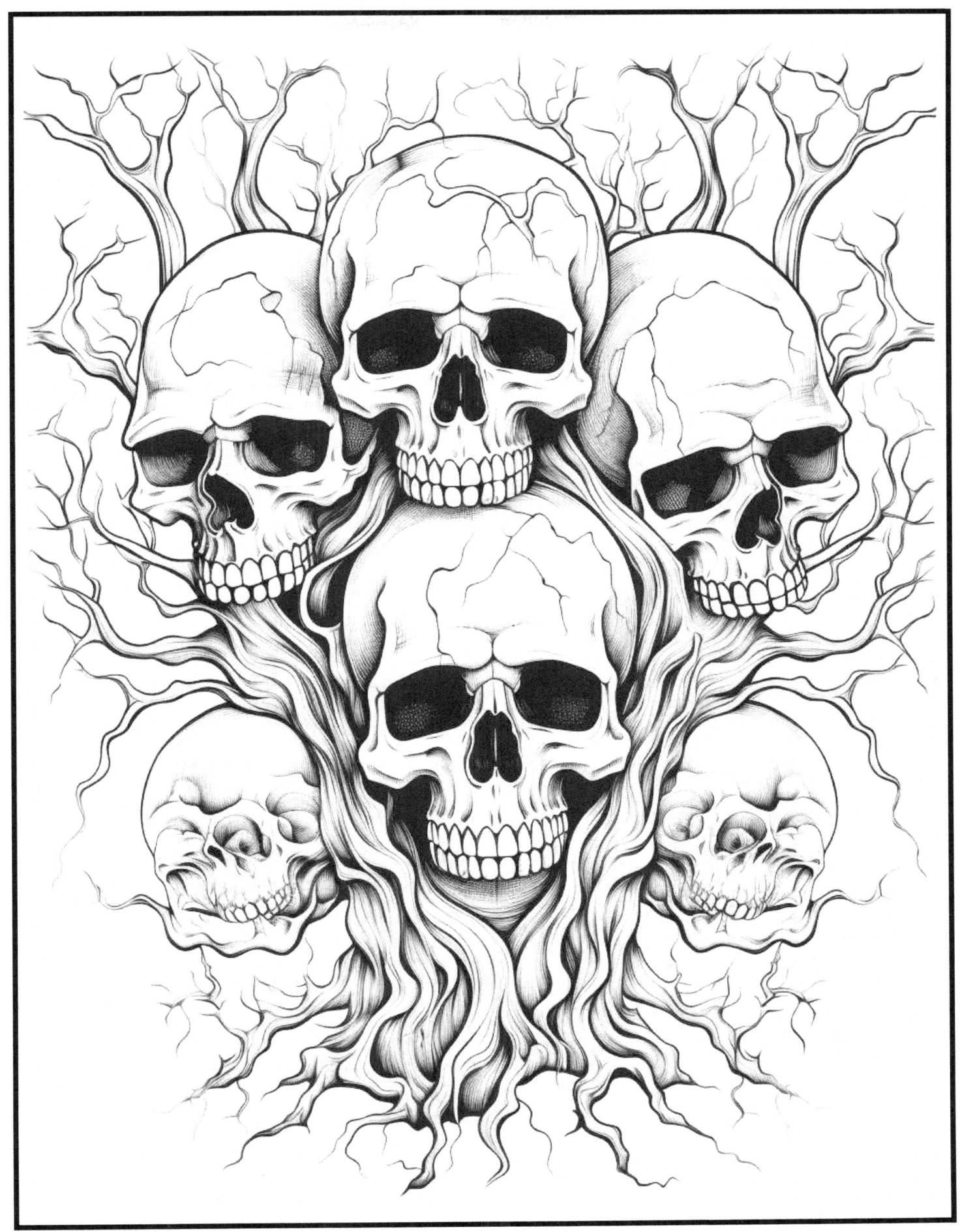

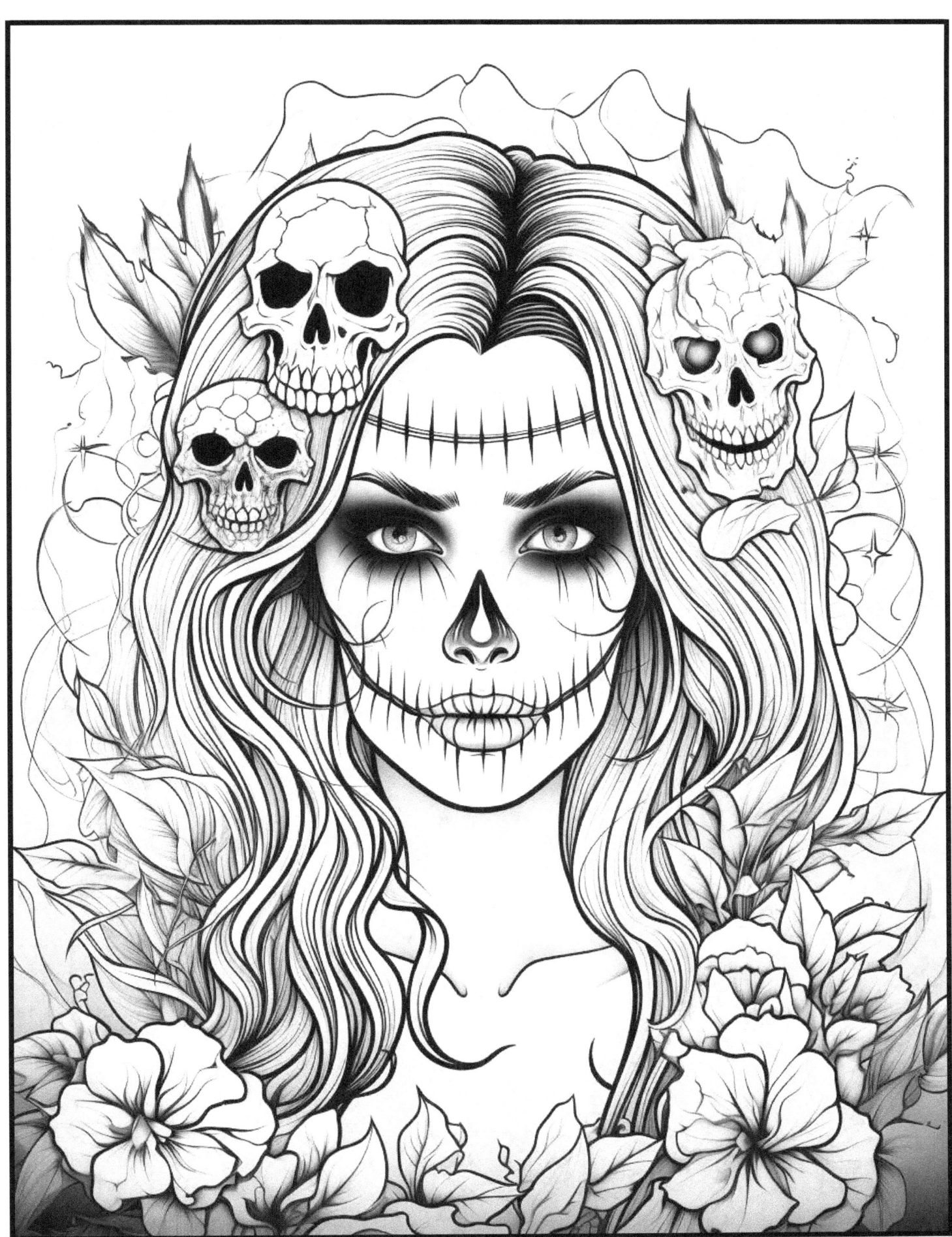

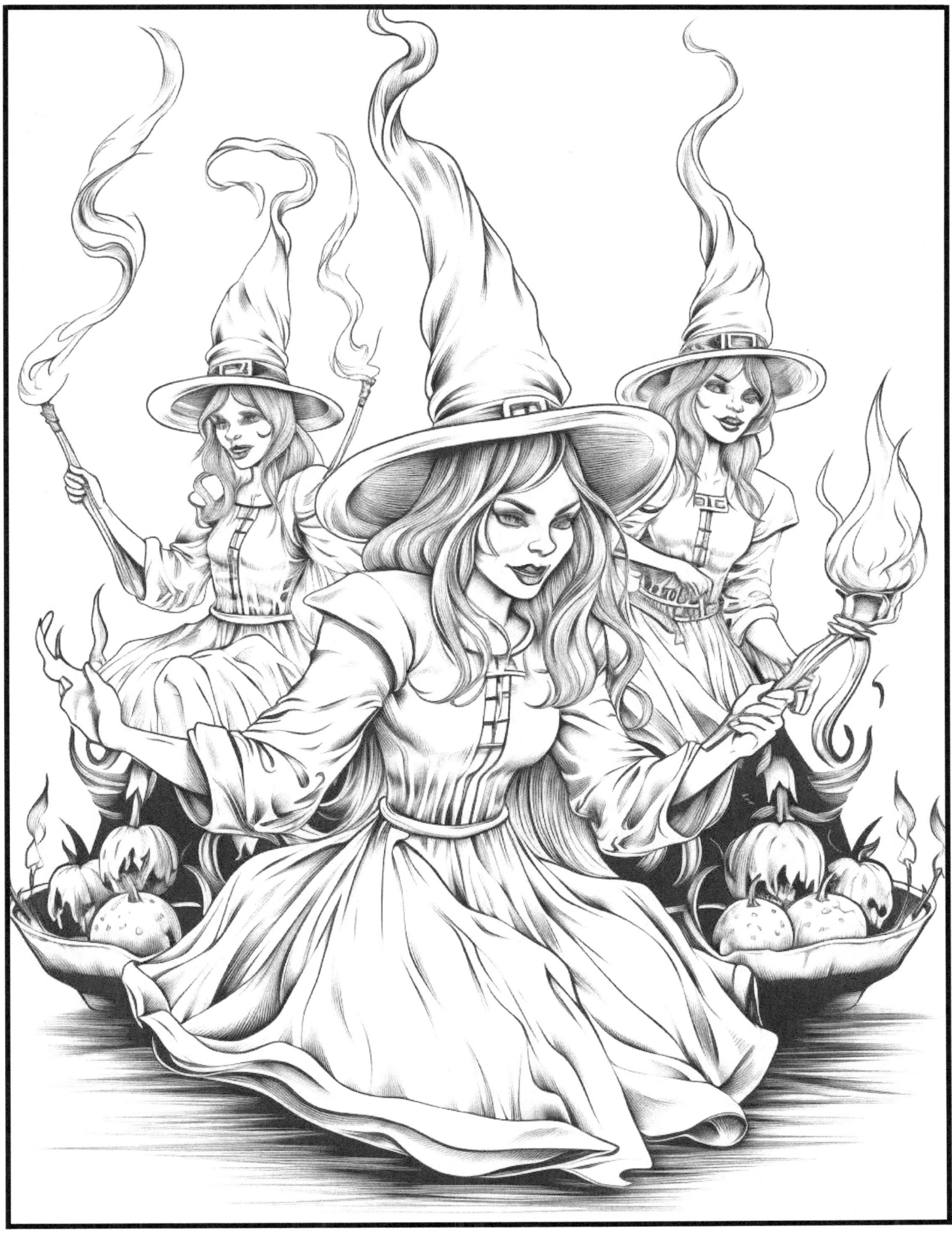

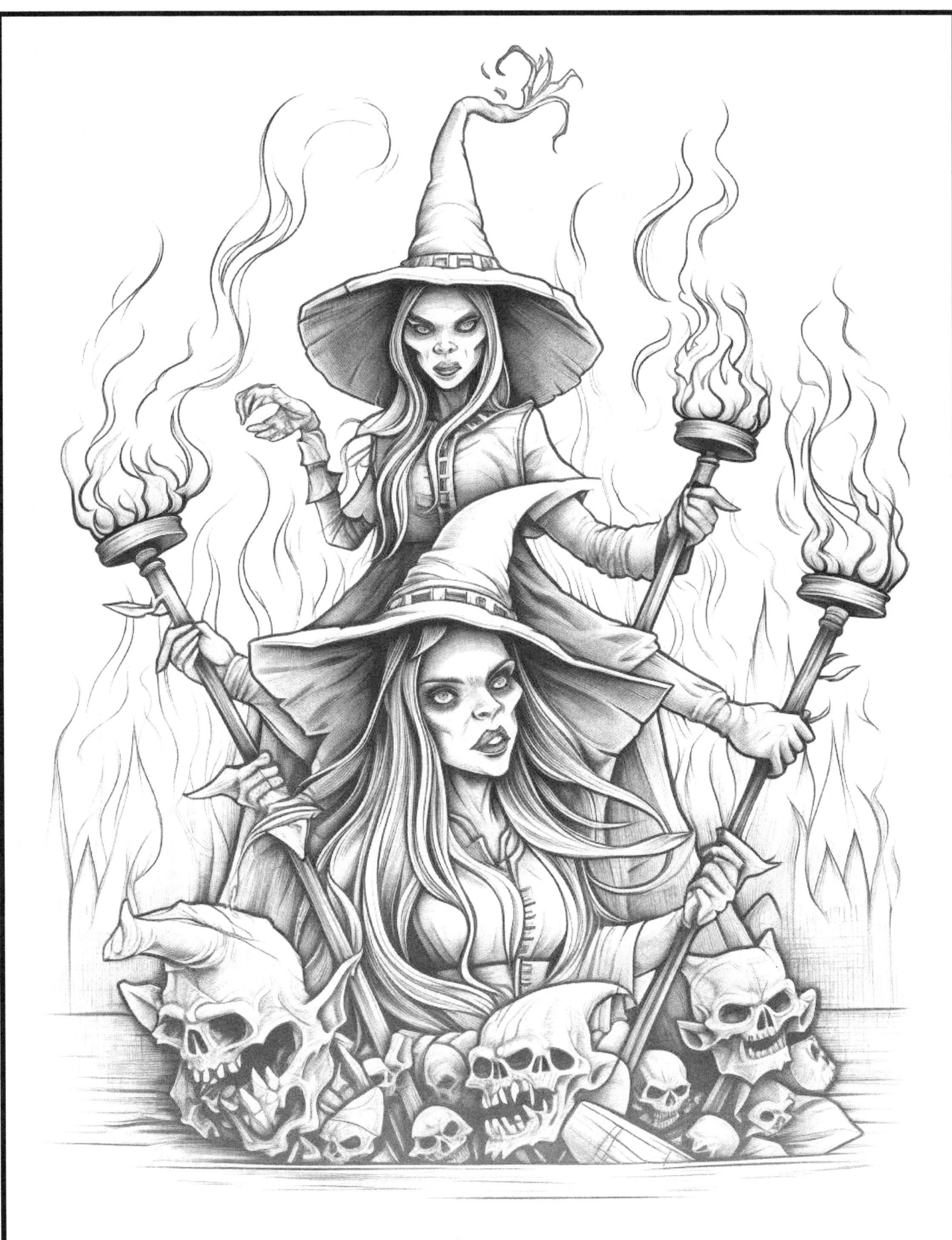

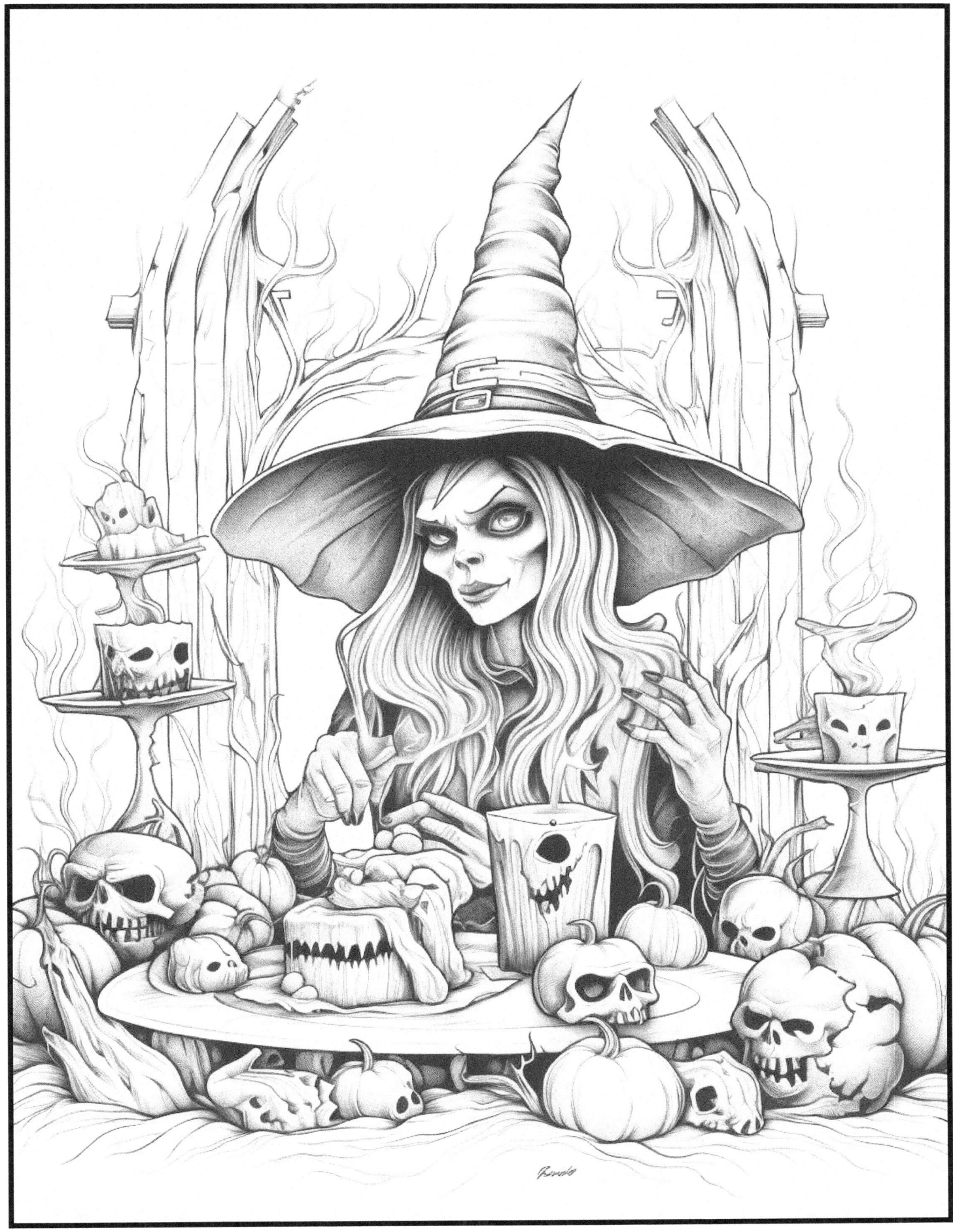

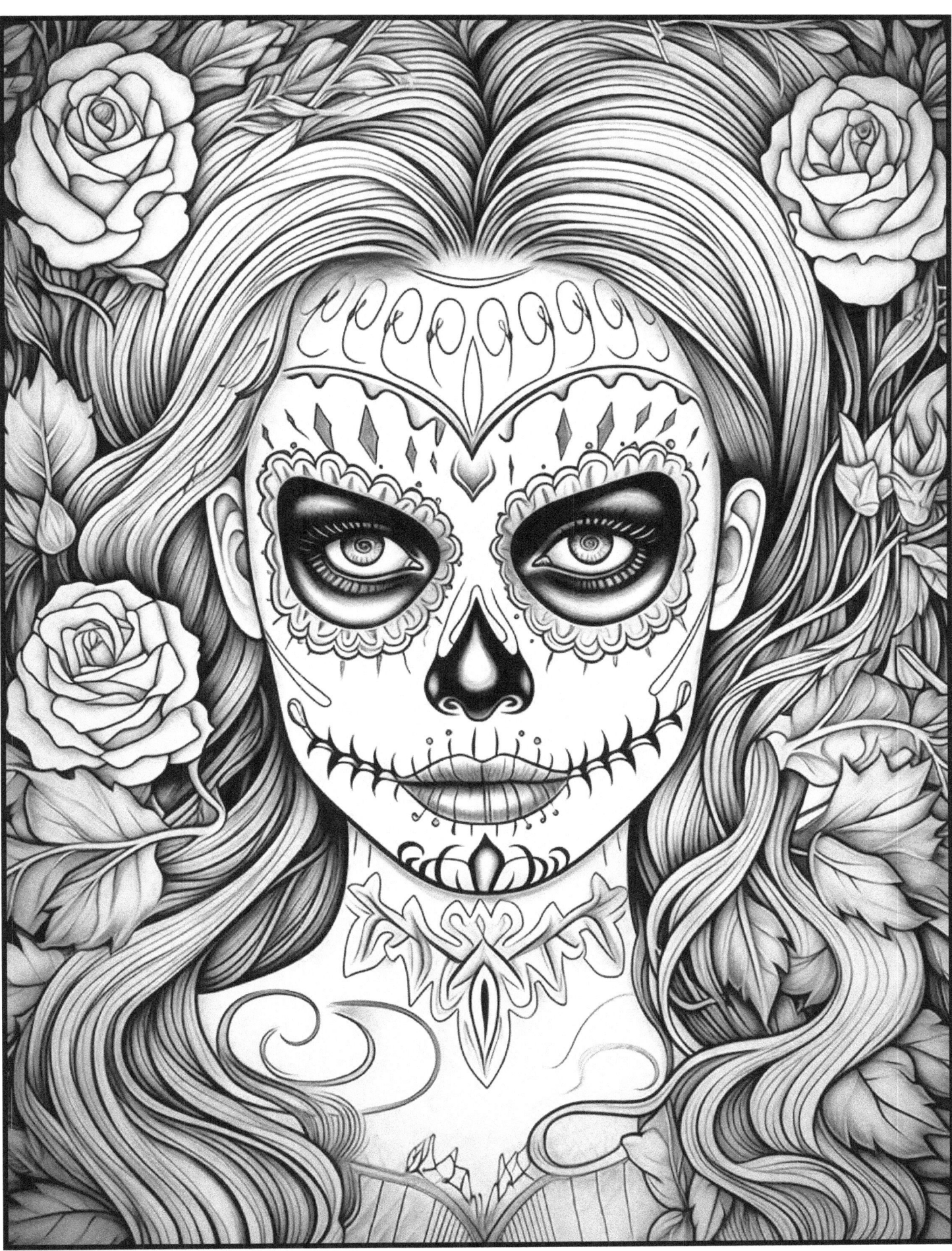

Dedicated to all those who love to immerse themselves in the dark magic of Halloween.